SCOTTISH DATES

Brian D. Osborne
and Ronald Armstrong

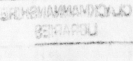

Birlinn

First published in Great Britain, 1996, by
Birlinn Limited
14 High Street
Edinburgh EH1 1TE

© Brian D. Osborne and Ronald Armstrong, 1996

The moral right of the authors has been asserted.

British Library Cataloguing-in-Publication Data
A Catalogue record of this book is available
from the British Library.

ISBN 1 874744 40 8

Designed and typeset in 10/11.5pt Bembo
by Janet Watson

Made and printed in Finland by
Werner Söderström OY

CONTENTS

Introduction 1

The Dates 2

Kings and Queens from
Kenneth MacAlpin 172

Scotland's Capital 175

Index 179

INTRODUCTION

Scottish Dates is a celebration of Scotland which we hope will interest and appeal to visitor and resident alike. Its aim is simple – to provide basic and accessible information on key moments and key personalities in Scotland's varied and colourful story.

The selection is unashamedly idiosyncratic, in the hope that what interests the authors may also interest, inform, entertain and even enlighten the reader. We have tried to remember that history is more than the story of kings, bloody battles, treaties and acts of parliaments. Bruce, Bannockburn and Bothwell Bridge appear but so also do Henry Bell, Byron, Blackwood's Magazine and the "Beautiful Railway Bridge of the Silv'ry Tay". If you have ever wanted to know how old was the "Auld Alliance", why we have Wade Roads or have difficulty distinguishing between the last wolf, General Wolfe and the Wolf of Badenoch, then we hope *Scottish Dates* will satisfy your curiosity or whet your interest to find out more about Scotland's story.

Each entry falls into three parts – a narrative account and an explanation of the wider significance or context of the person, event or movement, sandwiching a contemporary or near-contemporary view. This contemporary view section will, we hope, enable the reader to get a flavour of the period, a sense of the past and, perhaps, a benchmark against which to test the authors' views and conclusions. Most of the entries have been dealt with at uniform length – a handful of dates, which can in some sense be seen as critical or symbolic moments in our history, have been expanded to allow for a fuller or more discursive entry.

Brian D Osborne
Ronald Armstrong
Autumn 1995

THE BATTLE OF MONS GRAUPIUS

This, the first reasonably authenticated "date", or recorded event in the history of Scotland, was a battle fought sometime between 83 and 85 A.D. between the invading Roman forces under Agricola, Governor of Britain, and the native inhabitants. That the field of battle was in the Grampian area (possibly near Bennachie), that the smaller Roman forces inflicted grievous casualties on the Caledonians and that one of the Caledonian leaders was Calgacus (The Swordsman), we know from the pages of Tacitus, historian and son-in-law of Agricola.

The sole source for this and many other events of Agricola's campaigns, Tacitus naturally gives the Roman point of view. Conscious of his artistic role as chronicler he also gives us a Calgacus, who is a prototype of national heroes like Wallace and Bruce, and invents and puts into Calgacus's mouth a patriotic speech which comes ringing down the centuries.

THE CONTEMPORARY VIEW

There is now no nation beyond us, nothing save the billows and the rocks and the Romans, still more savage. . . Alone of all men they covet with equal rapacity the rich and the needy. Plunder, murder and robbery, under false pretences, they call "Empire" and when they make a wilderness they call it "Peace".

Tacitus, *Agricola*

THE WIDER VIEW

Agricola's army, after its victory, continued to the Moray Firth, while the Roman fleet moved up the coast and crossed to subdue the Orkneys. Agricola was recalled to Rome and the great legionary fortress at Inchtuthill, intended as the centre of Roman power in the north, was abandoned around 85 A.D. The Caledonians never repeated the tactical error of committing large forces in the field, but began a long process of raids and guerilla tactics which was to continue for a further three centuries.

THE BUILDING OF
THE ANTONINE WALL

The Roman Governor, Lollius Urbicus, developed the Emperor Hadrian's policy of containing the persistent raiding of the Caledonian tribes by building a "limes" or fixed frontier – in other words a wall – named this time after the Emperor Antoninus Pius. Unlike the stone-built Hadrian's Wall, constructed between 122 and 136, this wall was made of turf and stretched 37 miles from Bridgeness on the Forth to Old Kilpatrick on the Clyde. It had a smaller rampart than its southern counterpart, but a more formidable vallum or ditch, 40 feet wide and at least 12 feet deep, which can still be seen in several places on the Central isthmus. The wall was built by detachments from the three legions stationed in Britain. The permanent garrison was, however, found by auxiliary cohorts from various provinces of the Empire. These troops were stationed in 18 or 19 forts along the wall. The wall was abandoned around 154, re-occupied some years later and finally abandoned later in the century.

THE CONTEMPORARY VIEW

Lollius Urbicus, after driving back the barbarians, built another wall of turf

Capotilinus, *Vita Antonini Pii*

[The Maetae] live close to the wall which divides the island into two parts and the Caledonians next to them

Dio Cassius

For the emperor. . . a detachment of the Twentieth Legion Valeria Victrix built 3000 feet

Distance slab from Antonine Wall

THE WIDER VIEW

The Romans' strategy of a garrisoned frontier was not permanently sustained during their occupation. The occupying forces created a network of strong, strategically placed forts such as Inchtuthill, and carried out a series of punitive thrusts deep into barbarian territory. The Northern tribes retained the capacity to overwhelm Roman forces, as was shown by the "Barbarian Conspiracy" of 367 when the Picts and Scots combined to overrun the frontier.

THE DEATH OF ST NINIAN

The eighth century English historian, Bede, tells of Ninian's foundation of *Candida Casa*, the "White House", and the early years of Christianity in Scotland. Modern archaeological evidence suggests that *Candida Casa*, a building remarkable for being built of mortared stone with limewashed plaster, was as tradition suggests, situated at Whithorn in Galloway. From there Christian influence radiated out, although its extent can only be inferred. Ninian, a Briton who had received his calling at the French monastery of St Martin at Tours, journeyed throughout large parts of Scotland in pursuit of his mission, judging by place name and other evidence.

THE CONTEMPORARY VIEW

The Southern Picts who live on this side of the mountains had, it is said, long ago given up the error of idolatry and received the true faith through the preaching of the Word by that reverend and saintly man Bishop Nynia, a Briton by birth. His episcopal see is distinguished by the name and church of St Martin. . . This place, belonging to the province of the Berniceans, is commonly called "at the white house" inasmuch as he built there a church of stone in a manner unusual among the Britons.

Bede, *Historia Ecclesiastica*

THE WIDER VIEW

Paradoxically, neither Columba, who made the most celebrated or romantic impact, nor Andrew, who became the patron saint, has as good a claim as Ninian to true significance in the history of Christianity in Scotland. Ninian had probably secured a foothold for the faith, even in places in the north, more than a hundred years before Columba made his spectacular arrival on the west coast of Argyll. Ninian's church was abandoned around 550 but in the next century new Northumbrian rulers propagated Ninian's cult to reinforce their control over local population.

THE COMING OF THE SCOTS TO DÁL RIATA

People called Scots, from the northern part of Ireland, had been colonising western areas of Scotland for two or more centuries before the largely symbolic arrival of Fergus MacErc and his brothers Lorn and Angus from the Irish Dál Riata, a tale made much of in later records. The brothers were intent on extending Scots power in the new land and each of them founded kingdoms on the western seaboard – *Earra-ghaidheal* (Argyll) means coastland of the Gael. Fergus took Kintyre, Angus Islay and Jura, and Lorn the northern part, which still bears his name.

There were further divisions when Angus's grandsons Comgall and Gabhran held sway over Cowal and Knapdale respectively, but the Scots remained closely allied and pushed their sphere of influence east into Pictland, a move associated with the near-contemporary arrival of Christianity in these parts. The main strongholds of the Scots were Dunollie, near Oban and the strikingly situated rock fortress of Dunadd, near Crinan.

THE CONTEMPORARY VIEW

> *Three sons of Erc, the son of pleasant Eochaid, three men who got the blessing of Patrick, took Scotland – great were their deeds – Loarn, Fergus and Angus. Ten years Loarn, with distinguished renown, was in the Kingdom of Argyle. . .*

Duan Albanach

THE WIDER VIEW

So it was that these petty kings of Scots brought their name, a distinctive and vivid culture and a lasting political inheritance to Scotland. From Angus, in fact, sprang Somerled and the Lords of the Isles *(q.v.)*, while the royal house of a later, united, Scotland came from Gabhran. But it was the cultural and linguistic influence of the Gaels which was most enriching – the folklore of tales like Cuchullain and Fingal, and the immense influence of the Gaelic language on the place-name map of Scotland.

St Columba Comes to Iona

Although Christianity already had a foothold in Scotland when Columba landed on Iona after his fabled crossing from Ireland, the impact of his arrival was political as well as religious, not least because of his status as a prince of the Uí Néill. Iona, as an island base, was well situated for missionary work in the heavily indented west coast and among the Scots of Dál Riata. A beacon of civilisation and learning, Iona's influence gradually spread throughout the kingdoms of Alba and beyond. Columba's encounters with shadowy figures like Brude, King of Pictland, and tales of miracles testify to his saintliness but strain credulity. What is certain is that Columba and Iona represented an ideal of Celtic Christianity, which survived centuries of strife and retain a special place even today in Scotland's spiritual life.

The Contemporary View

At another time, when the Saint was obliged to cross the River Ness. . . [a] monster suddenly comes up and with a great roar rushes on him with open mouth. The Saint, after making the sign of the cross in the air and with his holy hand upraised, commanded the ferocious monster, saying, "Go no further!"

Adamnan, *Life of Columba* (c.690)

We were now treading that illustrious Island, which was once the luminary of the Caledonian regions, whence savage clans and roving barbarians derived the benefits of knowledge, and the blesssings of religion.

Samuel Johnson, *A Journey to the Western Islands.* (1775)

The Wider View

By the end of the seventh century all of the kingdoms of Alba were Christian, although the extent of Columba's contribution to this could be disputed. In Dál Riata, however, he inspired a self-confidence which led in time to a larger Alba, united under a King of Scots.

THE SYNOD OF WHITBY

In Scotland's formative years the boundaries between neighbouring states and the boundaries between religion and politics were equally fluid. The decision of King Oswiu of Northumbria to hold a church conference on the appropriate form of tonsure and the correct date for celebrating Easter may seem removed from the main line of Scottish history. There was, however, more at stake than simply a theological debate between the Columban Abbot Colmán and St Wilfrid. The decisions of the Synod of Whitby, by rejecting the Celtic traditions of the Columban church, also coincide with, and support, Oswiu's hegemonistic ambitions for northern Britain.

Oswiu was the son of Oswald, a convert to Christianity who had introduced Columban missionaries into Northumbria, whose bishopric of Lindisfarne had been subject to Iona. The decisions of the Synod, which imposed the conventions of Western Roman Chrisitianity, led to the Columban monks withdrawing from Northumbria and returning to Iona.

THE CONTEMPORARY VIEW

Colmán seeing that his doctrine was spurned and his sect despised took with him those who wished to follow him, – that is, those who refused to receive the Catholic Easter and the tonsure of the crown. . . and returned to Scotland to discuss what he should do regarding these things.

Bede, *Historia Ecclesiastica*

THE WIDER VIEW

Whitby marked the end of Columban influence in England. Oswiu probably saw adherence to mainstream Roman, rather than Irish or Columban ways, as having advantages in both his southwards ambitions – towards Mercia, and his successful attempts to assert overlordship in Pictland. This latter inevitably brought him and his son Ecgfrith into conflict with the Scottish kings of Dál Riata and the Strathclyde Britons, both of whom had sought, with varying degrees of success, by war and dynastic marriages, to control Pictland.

THE BATTLE OF NECHTANSMERE

The Scotland of the seventh century was a land of four kingdoms which, according to the sparse documentary evidence, were pretty constantly at war with each other. The famous victory of the Picts, under King Bridei, or Brude, over the Angles can be seen as a particular turning point. Nechtansmere, near Forfar in Angus, was a shattering blow to the expansionist Angles from Lothian and Northumbria, and the victors are seen by some as proto-Scottish nationalists. Little is known about the Picts, but their claims to the land certainly predated those of the expansionist Anglians who had moved against Strathclyde and Dál Riata. Bridei was a son of King Bili of Strathclyde. At Nechtansmere the invaders were emphatically repulsed, their King, Ecgfrith, perishing with most of his army.

THE CONTEMPORARY VIEW

For in the same year the same king who had rashly led an army to ravage the province of the Picts was led on by the enemy's feigning flight into the defiles of inaccessible mountains, and was killed along with the chief part of the troops which he had brought with him. . . And from this time the hope and valour of the kingdom of the Angles began to ebb, recede and sink, for both the Picts and the Scots who were in Britain recovered the land of their possession which the Angles held.

Bede, *Historia Ecclesiastica*

THE WIDER VIEW

The defeat of the Northumbrians did not represent a move towards a united Scotland. That was far in the future, though Bridei's Strathclyde origins emphasise the complex interconnections between the kingdoms. Nechtansmere produced a kind of equilibrium among the kingdoms by checking Anglian ambitions. It also helped to define the limits of the territory which would in time be called Scotland.

THE BOOK OF KELLS

"The chief relic of the Western World".

This, the finest flower of Celtic art and masterpiece of Celtic Christianity, is generally supposed to have had its genesis in the monks' scriptorium of Iona, St Columba's foundation, and was taken from there to Kells in County Meath, Ireland ("the great Gospel of Columcille" – The Annals of Ulster).

A Latin Gospel, made as a book for laying on the altar, it is the greatest and most elaborately illuminated of all the manuscripts of the Hiberno-Saxon tradition. It is believed that the work was completed in Kells, established in the early ninth century as a new centre for the monks of Iona.

The book was preserved for civilisation from the marauding Norse raiders by the foresight of the Columban monks. These Vikings ravaged Iona and its abbey five times in all, and left as a memory the name Martyrs' Bay, close to the present jetty on the island. The monks took the book to Kells as a haven from the dangerous western seaboard of Scotland, although Kells, 60 kilometres north-west of Dublin, was itself more than once the victim of "the fury of the Norseman".

Ever since the Scots from Northern Ireland had settled in what is now Argyll, the northern part of the island of Britain had been a land of four kingdoms. As well as the Scots of Dál Riata there were the Britons of Strathclyde, the Angles in the south-east and the Picts in the mountainous north and east. Now into this maelstrom of rival peoples had sailed the Norse from Scandinavia.

Within a decade or so the epicentre of Celtic Christianity had shifted to Dunkeld in Perthshire and later to St Andrews, and in a corresponding movement, political power was vested in Alba, a unified kingdom of Picts and Scots.

The relationship of the art of the illuminated gospels and contemporary creations in stone cannot be stated with certainty; however, some see the detailed and complex ornamentation of the great books as the inspiration for stone cross slabs "aswirl with curves and bosses and aesthetically very close to the well-known Chi-Rho page in the Book of Kells" (Bannerman).

In music, there is evidence from sculpture that the harp, or clarsach, was the principal instrument. Some cymbals and pipes would also be used, although the great Highland bagpipe did not appear until much later. Inferring from the other arts, the music was probably highly melodious and showed a fondness for decorated grace notes.

THE CONTEMPORARY VIEW

When the saint himself was chanting the evening hymn with a few of the brethren, as usual, outside the King's fortifications, some Druids, coming near to them, did all they could to prevent God's praises being sung in the midst of a pagan nation. On seeing this the saint began to sing the 44th psalm, and at the same moment so wonderfully loud, like pealing thunder, did his voice become, that king and people were struck with terror and amazement.

Adamnan, *Life of Columba (c.690)*

THE WIDER VIEW

Its travels and dangers over, the Book of Kells now resides in safety and security as the greatest treasure of Trinity College, Dublin – where little reference is made to its origins in Iona.

KENNETH MACALPIN, KING OF PICTS AND SCOTS

From this date, in the king lists of both kingdoms, Kenneth, High King of the Scots of Dál Riata, appears as leader of the Picts of the east as well. Although he had some prior claim to the Pictish throne, Kenneth probably won it in battle. Now all territory north of the Forth was ruled by one King of Alba and the "unification" of what we call Scotland had commenced. At that time, or shortly after, the capital shifted from Dunadd, near Crinan, to Forteviot in Strathearn, and in religious affairs, the influence of Dunkeld replaced that of Iona.

THE CONTEMPORARY VIEW

And in the seventh year of his reign – when Danish pirates had occupied the shores, and with the greatest slaughter had destroyed the Picts who defended their land – Kenneth passed over into. . . the remaining territories of the Picts. . . And so he was the first of the Scots to obtain the monarchy of the whole of Albania, which is now called Scotia. . .

Chronicle of the Canons of Huntingdon

THE WIDER VIEW

The races and kingdoms of Scotland were already interconnected but the union of 843 was driven by a real necessity – the unifying factor of the attacks of the Norsemen, the "fifth force" in the politics of the ninth century. Unifying factor, perhaps because the Norse onslaught on the western seaboard drove the Scots eastward, or perhaps because the Pictish kingdom was already weakened by attacks from the north.

In 937 a move by the new power of Alba against the "English" to the south was repulsed amid terrible slaughter at Brunanburgh. Although Edinburgh was held by the Alban kings from c.960, it was not until 1034 that the last independent state, Strathclyde, came into the expanded kingdom of Scotland.

THE BATTLE OF BRUNANBURH

Relations with the English kings gradually became more significant, as a change from the more usual internecine quarrels. The grandson of Kenneth MacAlpin *(q.v.)*, Constantine III, tried to seize the initiative, first of all around 915 when he led an army south, but the Scoto-Pict forces from Alba withdrew when the emergent power of the Wessex monarchy manifested itself.

The *Anglo-Saxon Chronicle* records that a few years later Constantine "with all his people", and the King of the Strathclyde Britons (who may have been his brother – an indication of the comparative unity of Scotland at this time) "chose" King Edward, Alfred's son, "for father and lord".

It was Edward's successor, Athelstan, whose forces attacked eastern Scotland by sea and by land, penetrating as far as the Mearns. Constantine, allied with Strathclyde and aided by Danes from Ireland under Anlaf, sought to give battle but was heavily defeated at Brunanburh, probably near the Solway.

THE CONTEMPORARY VIEW

In this year king Ethelstan, lord of earls, ring-giver to men, and his brother also prince Edmund won life-long glory in conflict with the sword's edges around Brunnanburgh. They clove the shield-wall, hewed the war-lindens with hammered blades. . . The foe gave way: the folk of the Scots and the ship-fleet fell death-doomed. . .
. . . the aged Constantin came north to his country by flight. . . bereft of his kinsmen. . . bereaved in the battle.

Anglo-Saxon Chronicle

THE WIDER VIEW

This stirring triumph song invests Brunanburh with immense significance. The battle terminated the expansionist ambitions of the MacAlpin dynasty. Alba sought friendship with England and sided with kings like Edmund against the Danes from Ireland. In 945 Malcolm I, King of Scots, is recorded as Edmund's "helper both on sea and land". Such a subservient position would be echoed in feudal times.

THE DEATH OF KING DUNCAN

Duncan I's accession in 1034 and his killing by Macbeth in 1040 gave Shakespeare the plot of Macbeth and exemplifies some of the problems of Scottish kingship. Succession was not strictly hereditary; a system known as "tanistry" passed the throne to an adult descendant or tanist of a previous king. This avoided minorities and enabled a competent monarch to be found in the Royal House. Duncan's predecessor, his grandfather Malcolm II, had killed off many of the tanists to ensure patrilineal succession for Duncan.

The surviving tanists were Macbeth and his wife Gruoch. Contrary to Shakespeare's version, derived from the inventive sixteenth century Scottish annalist Hector Boece, Duncan was a younger man than Macbeth, and unwilling to wait to inherit the crown. He rebelled against Duncan, killed him in battle and exiled his sons, Malcolm and Donald. In 1057/58 Malcolm returned and overthrew Macbeth and Macbeth's stepson and successor, Lulach.

THE CONTEMPORARY VIEW

Duncan, the king of Scotland, was killed in autumn. . . by his earl, Macbeth, Findlaech's son; who succeeded to the kingdom. . .
Chronicle of Marianus Scottus (c.1073)

Macbeth, Findlaech's son, reigned for seventeen years. And he was killed in Lumphanan, by Malcolm, Duncan's son; and was buried in the island of Iona.
Chronicles of the Kings of Scotland

THE WIDER VIEW

Scottish Kings had traditionally been the "ard righ" – the high king, but a king surrounded by a group of lesser sub-kings – the "mormaers" or earls, often related to the Royal House. This, combined with the system of tanistry, made a substantial number of people into potential king material. The sacrilegious horror with which Shakespeare invests Macbeth's murder of Duncan perhaps reflects a later age's social order and Shakespeare's eye to royal patronage rather than contemporary Scottish views.

THE DEATH OF THORFINN, EARL OF ORKNEY

The Norse invaders, whose coming had caused so much fear among the communities of Scotland and Ireland, established powerful semi-autonomous states and the rulers of the Norse earldom of Orkney were figures of more than local significance. The earldom was established late in the ninth century and produced figures like Magnus, murdered around 1117 and later canonised, and Thorfinn.

Thorfinn exemplifies the Norse influence and involvement in Scotland; his mother was a daughter of Malcolm II, while his daughter Ingibjord was to become the first wife of Malcolm III "Canmore". On Malcolm II's death, Thorfinn had a strong claim to the Scottish throne. He was involved in Macbeth's overthrow of Duncan and reputedly went with Macbeth on pilgrimage to Rome. He also endowed a cathedral for the Northern Isles at Birsay.

THE CONTEMPORARY VIEW

Earl Thorfinn, Sigurd's son, has been the noblest earl in the islands, and has had the greatest dominion, of all earls of the Orkneymen. He possessed Shetland and Orkney [and] the Hebrides; he had also a great dominion in Scotland and Ireland. . . Thorfinn was the greatest warrior. He took the earldom when he was five winters old, and he ruled for more than sixty winters.

Heimskringla, St. Olaf's Saga.

THE WIDER VIEW

Inter-marriage with the Scottish nobility eventually saw this Norse earldom pass into Scottish hands. In 1379 the Sinclair or St Clair family was granted possession by King Haakon Magnusson. The Sinclair Earls maintained the Norse sea-faring tradition, with Henry the first Earl voyaging to the Faeroes, Iceland, Greenland, and perhaps even as far as North America. Elsewhere in Scotland the St Clair's princely status was demonstrated by building the Gothic masterpiece of Rosslyn Chapel – founded in 1446 by William the third Earl.

THE DEATH OF ST MARGARET

Margaret, grand-daughter of King Edmund Ironside of England, was born while her father was in exile in Hungary. She came to Scotland after the Norman Conquest and in 1069 became the second wife of Malcolm Canmore (Malcolm III). Few women have had greater influence on Scottish religious and cultural life.

Margaret was cultured, deeply pious and intellectually committed to mainstream Catholicism. She found in Scotland remains of old and irregular practices and devoted herself to reform. The "five articles of Queen Margaret" – observance of Sunday rest, the timing of the Lenten fast, regularisation of the Mass, a ban on marriage within forbidden degrees and regularity of communion – helped bring Scotland into line with Latin Christianity. The Queen, however, also cherished the Culdees, the religious communities of the Celtic Church. Her ancestry inclined her to take a more elevated view of kingship than had been the Scottish custom.

THE CONTEMPORARY VIEW

She instituted also more ceremonious service of the king, so that when he walked or rode he was surrounded with great honour by many troops. . . The Queen endeavoured to venerate and love Christ in them [the Culdees] and to visit them very often with her presence and conversation. . .other things too, which had sprung up contrary to the rule of faith and the statutes of ecclesiastical observances, she took pains to condemn. . .

Prior Turgot of Durham, *Life of Queen Margaret (c. 1100)*

THE WIDER VIEW

Margaret opened up Scottish Christianity to southern and European influences, a process continued by her three sons who became kings, most notably by David I. She symbolises increasing Scottish involvement with England, at the expense of the traditional links with Scandinavia. Her personal piety was recognised by her canonisation in 1251; the only Scottish royal saint.

THE ACCESSION OF KING DAVID I

David, the youngest son of Malcolm Canmore and Margaret, was the third of their children to become King. He was educated at the English court, where his sister Matilda was Henry I's queen. In 1113 he had, through marriage, become Earl of Huntingdon, a title for which he paid feudal homage to the King of England, opening up a long-term problem of the distinction between due homage for the Scottish king's English lands and the independence of the Scottish throne.

David's reign was marked by strongly Norman and modernising influences. Feudalism was developed and settlement by French and English knights encouraged; families such as the Bruces of Annandale and the Stewarts were planted in Scotland at this period. Royal control over the administration of justice was strengthened, burghs were established, for example at Edinburgh, Berwick and Roxburgh, and his mother's work on church reform continued. It was in the church that David's most visible impact was seen; he founded more than twenty religious houses including the Cistercian abbey of Melrose and the Augustinian abbeys of Holyrood and Jedburgh.

THE CONTEMPORARY VIEW

King David was a very pious man. . . zealous in restoring churches...
During his reign many monasteries were restored, and indeed built from
foundations. . . All these. . . this most pious king David adorned with
great weights of gold and silver and. . . precious jewels. . .
                              Chronicles of the Kings of Scotland

A sair sanct for the croun
                    Attributed to King James I (1394–1437) and
                    referring to David's generosity to the Church

THE WIDER VIEW

David's reign saw an increase in the power and influence of the Scottish kings; he had learned much from his stay at the Court of Henry I. His religious benefactions, while reflecting his personal piety, also reflected his campaign to bring Scotland into the European mainstream.

THE BATTLE OF THE STANDARD

Landholding and feudal ties in England often embroiled Scots kings in English wars. On the death of Henry I of England, a civil war broke out between supporters of his daughter Maud, widow of the Holy Roman Emperor, and her cousin Stephen, who seized the throne. David I had sworn fealty to Maud (for his English estate of the Honour of Huntingdon) and in 1138, after some dealings with Stephen, invaded Northumberland in support of the Empress Maud. David's real objective was to secure Cumbria and Northumberland for the Scottish crown. While his army was devastating Northumbria, Stephen's forces were performing similar outrages in the Lothians.

Later in 1138 David assembled a large army and pressed south towards Yorkshire. On 22 August at Cowton Moor, near Northallerton, David's army was comprehensively deafeated in a battle which has come to be known as "The Battle of the Standard", from the wagon with the banner of St Peter of York, which the English commander, Archbishop Thurston, brought on to the field.

THE CONTEMPORARY VIEW

In the year 1138, king David miserably wasted the whole of Northumbria.

Chronicle of Melrose

In the summer, king David again crossed the river Tees. And the English army met him on Cowton Moor. . . The Scots were conquered, many being captured, and many killed.

Chronicle of Huntingdon

THE WIDER VIEW

Despite defeat David managed, in the Treaty of Durham (1139), to gain control, through his son, of the Earldom of Northumberland. This, with the Scottish possession of Cumbria, gave David mastery of much of northern England. David was one of the most innovative and effective Scottish kings, his reign marks the accomplishment of feudalism and a secure dynastic succession. King and realm increasingly attracted notice and admiration throughout Europe.

THE DEATH OF SOMERLED

In the complex world of twelfth century Scotland the figure of Somerled, the semi-autonomous sub-king of Argyll, stands out for his long fight against the Norse invader and equally for his assertion of independence against the Scottish Kings David I and Malcolm IV.

Somerled probably came of mixed stock, possibly having a Norse mother while his father Gillebride, came of the royal house of Dalriada. In the 1150s he fought a series of battles against the Norse invaders, culminating in a sea battle off Islay in 1156, in which his fleet of small and manoeuvrable galleys equipped with the newly introduced rudder (as opposed to the Viking steering oar), defeated the forces of the Norse king Godred. Somerled rebelled against Malcolm, but concluded a peace in 1160. In 1164, in the words of the Chronicle of Man "wishing to subdue all Scotland to himself", he invaded the mainland with 160 galleys and was killed at Renfrew. Somerled founded Saddell Abbey in Kintyre and is buried there.

THE CONTEMPORARY VIEW

Somerled, the regulus of Argyle, wickedly rebelling for now twelve years against Malcolm, the King of Scots, his natural lord, after he had landed at Renfrew, bringing a large army from Ireland and various places, was at last through divine vengeance slain there, along with his son, and innumerable people. . .

Chronicle of Melrose

THE WIDER VIEW

Somerled's dominance of the southern Hebrides died with him. His lands were divided between his surviving sons. His grandson, Donald of Islay, gave his name to Clan Donald. Donald's grandson, Angus Og, supported Bruce in the Wars of Independence and gained wide estates. Angus's son John assumed the title of Lord of the Isles, held by Somerled's descendants until its forfeiture in 1493 *(q.v.)*.

KING HAAKON IV's EXPEDITION TO THE WESTERN ISLES

The Western seaboard presented a continuing problem for Scottish kings of the twelfth and thirteenth centuries – the islands were held by the Norse kings and the mainland barely acknowledged fealty to Scotland. Alexander III *(q.v.)* tried to buy out the Norwegian title to the Isles but Haakon IV resolved to reassert his claim to the west. With his allies, Magnus, King of Man, and the lords of the Western Isles, he assembled a strong fleet. A raiding party sailed up Loch Long, dragged ships overland and sailed down Loch Lomond to plunder the Lennox.

On 1st October Haakon and the main part of his fleet was lying at anchor at Largs. Some ships were driven on shore by strong winds and their crews and later their rescuers forced into battle with a sizeable Scottish army. Short of supplies and far from their base the Norwegian force withdrew.

THE CONTEMPORARY VIEW

. . . they took their boats, and drew them up to a large lake, which is called Loch Lomond. Out across the lake lay a county that is called Lennox. There are also very many islands in that lake, and well-inhabited. The Norwegians wasted these islands with fire. They burned also all the dwellings all around the lake, . . .

Frisbok's Hakon Hakon's Son's Saga

THE WIDER VIEW

The Battle of Largs, though a fairly minor engagement, saw the end of Norse power in Scotland. The island chieftains had proved to be unwilling allies to Haakon and the struggle to rule these distant islands came to be seen as futile. Haakon's successor Magnus, in the Treaty of Perth (1266), sold Man and the Western islands to Scotland. The last Norse possessions, Orkney and Shetland, came to the Scottish crown in 1470 as an unredeemed pledge for a royal dowry.

THE DEATH OF ALEXANDER III, KING OF SCOTS

On a fiercely stormy night in March 1286 King Alexander III, hastening along the Fife coast to his second wife, Joleta or Yolande, fell from his horse and broke his neck. Alexander's children by his first marriage, to Margaret Plantagenet, were all dead. His heir was an infant grand-daughter, Margaret, daughter of Eric of Norway – an unsatisfactory situation in a troubled age. Anxiety for a male heir had motivated Alexander's remarriage and his dangerous journey from Edinburgh to Kingsburgh was driven by both a personal and dynastic need to be with his new wife.

Alexander came to the throne at the age of eight in 1249 and his reign had seen a series of struggles to defend the Scottish throne and church from English claims to overlordship. He held extensive estates in England and did feudal homage for these estates – a process Henry III and Edward I of England attempted to convert into recognition of their self-proclaimed title to supremacy over Scotland.

THE CONTEMPORARY VIEW

One of the earliest surviving pieces of Scots verse, an anonymous work of the fourteenth century, comments on Alexander's death and its consequences :

Quhen Alexander our kynge was dede,
That Scotlande lede in lauche and le,
Away was sons of alle and brede,
Off wyne and wax, of gamyn and gle.
Our golde was changit in to lede.
Crist, borne in virgynyte,
Succoure Scotlande, and ramede,
That is stade in perplexite.

THE WIDER VIEW

Alexander's reign had been successful – the Norse threat neutralised, English pretensions resisted, the nation united, the economy strong. His death, followed by the death of the infant Maid of Norway in 1390, plunged Scotland into an internecine power struggle and series of English wars that only ended with victory at Bannockburn *(q.v.)*

TREATY OF SALISBURY

Alexander III's death in 1286 *(q.v.)* left the succession uncertain; the Queen was reportedly pregnant and a posthumous male heir would take precedence over Margaret, the Maid of Norway. Guardians were appointed to rule and supervise the succession. The Bruces and the Baliols claimed the crown through descent from David I and the Bruces pushed their claim to the point of civil war. Joleta's pregnancy proved false. The Guardians turned to an outside power to break the deadlock.

Edward I of England was both a skilled diplomat and the father of a potential husband for the Maid. The Treaty of Salisbury (6 November 1289) was the first step. It arranged for the Maid to leave Norway under Edward's protection and for him to send her into Scotland when the country was at peace. A dynastic marriage would hopefully secure a lasting peace.

Negotiations continued and in July 1290 a marriage treaty between the Maid and the Prince of Wales, Edward of Caernarvon, was signed at Birgham. The Scots understanding was that Scotland's independence should be secured, even if she eventually shared a sovereign with England, while Edward's goal was to incorporate Scotland into England.

THE CONTEMPORARY VIEW

[Scotland should] *remain separate and divided from England according to its rightful boundaries, free in itself and without subjection*

Treaty of Birgham

THE WIDER VIEW

The marriage plan failed due to the untimely death of the Maid of Norway. The Treaties of Salisbury and Birgham were ill-judged in that they admitted Edward's right to interfere in Scotland without defining the source of that right. The Scots' view was that he had been involved as neighbour and kinsman of the Maid, while Edward gratefully used it as further evidence of his role as feudal overlord.

FRANCO-SCOTTISH TREATY: "THE AULD ALLIANCE"

In 1292 the vacant Scottish throne was filled by King Edward's adjudication in favour of John Balliol. Balliol's unhappy reign began with his swearing fealty to Edward and ended in 1296 with his surrender to an invading English army – the derisive nickname of "Toom Tabard" was applied to him, reflecting the belief that he had merely the outward trappings of a King, without any of the necessary inner qualities.

In 1294 war between England and France prompted Edward to demand military support from Scotland, including the personal service of the King. The Scottish magnates determined to prevent Balliol obeying Edward's instructions; in an orderly revolution the Parliament held at Stirling in July 1295 overturned Balliol's government and appointed a ruling Council of 12 peers and bishops. Viewing an English war as inevitable the Council swiftly sought an alliance with France. France had been Scotland's natural ally against England for over two centuries but the treaty signed with Philip IV in Paris in October 1295 formalised this relationship. It did not, however, prevent Philip signing a separate peace with England in 1303.

THE CONTEMPORARY VIEW

. . . in good faith as loyal allies. . . the kings of France will aid and counsel the kings of Scotland to the best of their power. . .
Treaty of Corbeil

THE WIDER VIEW

The Treaty of 1295 was confirmed by King Robert I in the Treaty of Corbeil of 1326, providing an assurance of support for Scotland and a continuing involvement of Scotland in European wars as the treaty was regularly renewed. The alliance created in 1295, strengthened in 1326, formed the lynch-pin of Scottish foreign policy down to the post-Reformation Treaty of Edinburgh in 1560, and had important cultural, economic and social consequences as well as military and diplomatic effects. The active help of French troops was obtained on numerous occasions, even if the French visitors did not always appreciate the pleasures of campaigning in Scotland, as the following extract from a chronicler of a French army assisting Robert II in 1385 suggests.

The Contemporary View

*When these barons and knights of France, who had been used to
handsome hotels, ornamented apartments, and castles with good soft beds
to repose on saw themselves in such poverty, they began to laugh and to
say "What could have brought us hither? We have never known till now
what was meant by poverty and hard living."*

Jean Froissart

The Auld Alliance was a fully reciprocal treaty; Scots fought in France
on many occasions – perhaps most notably in the army of Joan of
Arc that relieved the city of Orleans in 1429 and which found itself
being welcomed to that city by its Scottish-born Bishop, John de
Kirkmichael. The Kings of France established the Scots Guard – the
Garde Ecossaise – as their personal bodyguard, an elite force that
continued in being down to the time of the Revolution. The Scots'
military tradition in France continued to be significant even after that
date – one of Napoleon's marshals, Jacques MacDonald, the Duke of
Taranto, being the son of a Scots Jacobite emigré.

Scotland's price for the treaty of 1295 was a commitment to invade
England. The feudal Scottish army mustered near Selkirk in March
1296 and was crushed by the highly professional English force at
Dunbar on 27 April. In the interim Edward had captured and sacked
Scotland's richest burgh, Berwick. The War of Independence had
started badly.

THE BATTLE OF STIRLING BRIDGE

After his victory at Dunbar, Edward I marched through Scotland as far north as Elgin crushing all opposition. In August 1296 at Berwick he secured the allegiance of Scotland's leading landowners and churchmen. In May 1297 there was a widespread popular rising against the English administration. Prominent in this rising was William Wallace, the younger son of a Renfrewshire knight who, with Andrew Murray, was able to raise an army of foot-soldiers from the feudal hosts of the earldoms of Scotland.

In September 1297 an English army, strong in cavalry and archers, under John de Warenne and Hugh Cressingham, arrived at the strategically important crossing of the Forth at Stirling. Neglecting to send a flanking force up-river, the English attacked across the narrow bridge. When part of the English army had crossed, Wallace ordered his foot to attack and the English vanguard was cut-off and massacred. Cressingham had crossed in the van and was killed, Warenne stayed with the main force and made a hurried escape to Berwick.

THE CONTEMPORARY VIEW

Till Stryvelyne this Willame Walays past:
And at the Bryg off Forth Willame
The Walays met with Karssyngame. . .
Thare Karssyngame at the last
Wyth the mast part off his men
Slayne besyd that bryg was then.
   Andrew of Wyntoun, *Orygynale Cronykil of Scotland (c. 1400)*

THE WIDER VIEW

The defeat of a professional knightly cavalry army by a semi-amateur Scottish infantry force was a shocking reversal of roles. Stirling Bridge's importance was not in permanent strategic gain – the English returned – but in the morale value of proving that they could be beaten, if the Scots fought on ground and with tactics that favoured them. In the spring of 1298 Wallace, by this time knighted, was appointed as Guardian of the Realm.

THE EXECUTION OF WILLIAM WALLACE

Wallace's second great battle, Falkirk, in July 1298 was a disaster resulting from the Scottish army being forced into pitched battle with the English military machine. Wallace resigned the Guardianship, and later travelled abroad seeking support for the Scottish cause. He returned in 1303 and engaged in guerilla warfare. In 1305 he was captured at Robroyston, north of Glasgow, by followers of Sir John Menteith, Edward's Keeper of Dumbarton Castle.

Wallace was transported to London and tried in Westminster Hall for treason and sundry other crimes, including the murder of Hesilrig, the sheriff of Lanark, in 1297. Wallace denied only the treason charge, arguing that he had never sworn fealty to Edward (his name being absent from the 1296 roll of submissions at Berwick). Edward's vengeance was not to be diverted by such technicalities. Wallace was found guilty of treason and executed on 23 August. He was hung, cut down whilst alive, disembowelled and finally beheaded. The four quarters of his body were displayed in Newcastle, Berwick, Stirling and Perth, while his head was mounted on London Bridge.

THE CONTEMPORARY VIEW

Allace, Scotland, to quhom sall thow compleyn!
Allace, fra payn qhua sall the now restreyn!

Allace, thow has now lost thi gyd off lycht!
Allace, quha sall defend the in thi richt?
Blind Harry's *Wallace*

THE WIDER VIEW

Wallace's death provided a potent martyr image which was to be as powerful a force as his leadership of the Scottish army had been. Wallace has been seen as a more democratic or proletarian leader than Bruce, however he worked within the same feudal society as the future King and showed no signs of questioning or rejecting it – the true distinction perhaps lying in Wallace's undeviating constancy towards the national cause.

THE CORONATION OF ROBERT THE BRUCE

Robert Bruce, Earl of Carrick, was the grandson of Robert Bruce "the Competitor" who had claimed the throne on the Maid of Norway's death. Bruce fought on the patriotic side in the rising of 1297, becoming joint Guardian of Scotland in 1298 after Wallace's resignation. Bruce resigned his Guardianship in 1300 and submitted to Edward in 1302. By 1305 Scottish resistance was almost broken; the deposed Balliol exiled, Edward planning a constitution for Scotland to confirm its status as a conquered province.

On 10 February 1306, Bruce invited John Comyn of Badenoch to Greyfriars Church, Dumfries, possibly to discuss a pact whereby Bruce would seize the Crown, with Comyn support being bought by the transfer of Bruce's lands. However the meeting ended in Bruce murdering Comyn.

Bruce made for Scone, where on 25 March he was crowned in the presence of just three bishops and four earls. Another ceremony two days later enabled the sister of the absent Earl of Fife (in England under Edward's control) to exercise her family's traditional privilege of installing Kings of Scots.

THE CONTEMPORARY VIEW

The Lord the Bruce to Glasgow raid,
And send about him, quhill he haid
Off his friendis a gret menyi.
And syne to Scone in hy raid he
And wes maid King but langir let,
And in the Kingis stole was set;
    John Barbour, *The Bruce (c. 1375)*

THE WIDER VIEW

Bruce's genealogical claim to the throne was legitimate. His constancy in the patriotic cause and moral right to national leadership was less marked than the Comyn's. Bruce's coup d'état needed either Comyn support or their neutralisation.

The coronation showed the extent of Scotland's division with most of the prelates and magnates either under Edward's control or opposed to Bruce.

THE BATTLE OF BANNOCKBURN

The journey from Scone in 1306 *(q.v.)* to Bannockburn was a long one for King Robert. He was defeated by the English commander Aymer de Valence at Methven in June 1306 and by John Macdougall in Strathfillan in August; he became a hunted fugitive, and fled to Ulster. On his return in 1307 he adopted the technique of hit and run guerilla warfare, avoiding set-piece confrontations, ignoring the conventions of chivalry and knightly conduct. Two years of brilliant campaigning against English garrisons and disaffected Scots, such as the Comyns and the Macdougalls of Argyll, secured much of Scotland for Bruce.

By March 1309 he was secure enough to be able to call his first parliament. Increasingly the country rallied to his support and the war was carried to England. Bruce and his lieutenants such as James Douglas and Thomas Randolph began to recapture the castles occupied by the English in 1306. The Scots lacking seige weapons most were captured by surprise and daring as at Perth in January 1313, when Bruce led a night assault scaling the castle walls with rope ladders.

By 1314 five major castles, including Stirling, remained in English hands. Bruce's brother had agreed with the governor of Stirling, Sir Philip Moubray, that if Stirling were not relieved by midsummer 1314 it would be surrendered. This arrangement guaranteed that Edward II, if only for prestige's sake, would invade. It forced a set-piece battle against an inevitably larger and better equipped army. Edward Bruce's foolish pact brought eight years of patient struggle to a desperate crisis.

Edward II was not the military leader his father had been but the English army had skilled and experienced commanders. Some 15,000 English infantry and 2,500 armoured cavalry were confronted near Stirling by some 8,000 Scottish foot and a small force of light horse. Bruce deployed his infantry in four brigades, mostly spearmen formed into hedgehog-like formations called schiltrons. The Scots as usual lacked archers. In the two days of battle (23/24 June 1314) the Scottish infantry proved that they could not only resist the assault of heavily armoured English cavalry but could manouevre and attack. The incident on the 23rd, in which Bruce engaged in single-handed combat with Sir Henry de Bohun, provides an enduring image of Bannockburn and the hero King. Bruce's victory over Bohun must have boosted his troops' morale, however undesirable it might be for the embodiment of the nation to engage in hand to hand combat.

Barbour gives the King's address to his troops on the eve of battle:

THE CONTEMPORARY VIEW

For we have thre gret avantage.
The first is, that we haf the richt;
And for the richt ilk man suld ficht.
The tothir is, thai ar cummyn heir,
For lypnyng[1] in thair gret power,
To seik us in our awne land. . .

The thrid is, that we for our lyvis
And for our childer and our wifis
And for the fredome of our land,
Ar strenyeit[2] in battle for to stand. . .

John Barbour, *The Bruce*

THE WIDER VIEW

Edward fled south, defeat turned into rout, but victory was not total. Bruce lacked cavalry to pursue the fleeing foe. Had Edward been captured, a peace could have been enforced and independence acknowledged. As it was another 14 years of war ensued before Edward III in the Treaties of Northampton and Edinburgh recognised the independence and integrity of Scotland and its traditional boundaries. Bannockburn, the greatest Scottish feat of arms, has its true importance in ending internal opposition to Bruce and re-creating the Scottish nation and national unity.

[1] trusting
[2] forced

THE BIRTH OF ROBERT STEWART

A vital concern for any medieval monarch was the succession to the throne – Scotland's turmoil after the death of Alexander III was proof of this. Robert the Bruce had a daughter, Marjorie, by his first wife, Isabel of Mar. Bruce was remarried in 1302 to Elizabeth de Burgh, daughter of the earl of Ulster and from this marriage came David born in 1324. David succeeded his father, reigning as David II from 1329-1371 but although twice-married had no legitimate heirs.

The succession then reverted to Marjorie's son, Robert. She had married Walter, the son of James the Stewart, who succeeded his father in the powerful office of Hereditary Steward of Scotland. Marjorie had a riding accident near Paisley in March 1316 and died giving birth to her first child, who, 55 years later, came to the throne as Robert II.

THE CONTEMPORARY VIEW

. . .if it happened (which God forbid) that the said lord King closed the last day of his life without any male heir begotten of his body, the noble man Lord Edward de Brus, brother of the King, as a vigorous man and as most highly skilled in warfare for the defence of the right and liberty of the kingdom of Scotland. . . shall succeed the said lord king. . .

Acts of the Parliaments of Scotland 1315

It cam with a lass and it will gang with a lass

James V on the Stewart Dynasty

THE WIDER VIEW

Parliament in 1315 set aside the normal rules of succession – Marjorie and her heirs would only succeed if the Bruce and Edward died without male heirs. However Edward Bruce died in 1318 and Parliament then changed the succession to favour the infant Robert, thus creating the Royal House of Stewart.

THE DECLARATION OF ARBROATH

Bannockburn did not bring peace; Edward II's claim to overlordship of Scotland remained active. Bruce rejected a papal truce in 1317 because it would prevent his recapturing Berwick. In 1319 and 1320 papal bulls excommunicated Bruce and his supporters and placed all Scotland under interdict – in theory no religious services could be held, but the Scottish bishops ignored the ban.

A reply, dated at "the monastery of Arbroath, in Scotland, April 6th" was sent to Pope John XXII on behalf of the "community of the realm of Scotland".

This has become known as the Declaration of Arbroath. Its principal author was probably Bernard of Linton, abbot of Arbroath and Chancellor of Scotland. In terse and brilliant language it tells of Edward's attacks and outrages "sparing neither age nor sex nor religious order", how Bruce heroically freed his people "like another Joshua or Maccabeus", pledges allegiance to Robert so long as he adheres to the principles of national independence but warns that were he to betray Scotland's independence they would "expel him as our enemy".

THE CONTEMPORARY VIEW

For as long as one hundred men remain alive, we shall never under any conditions submit to the domination of the English. It is not for glory or riches or honours that we fight, but only for liberty, which no good man will consent to lose but with his life.
            Declaration of Arbroath (Lord Cooper's translation)

THE WIDER VIEW

The excommunication and interdict were not lifted, and little was done to persuade Edward to sign a peace treaty. The Declaration had perhaps little practical value but it lives as the clearest and noblest statement of Scottish national feeling and with its fiercely conditional loyalty to the King reads as a remarkably "modern" and democratic document.

THE WOLF OF BADENOCH BURNS ELGIN CATHEDRAL

The career of Alexander Stewart (c1342-1406), the "Wolf of Badenoch", shows the problems Scottish kings had in ruling the Highlands and the power of the great barons. The fourth son of King Robert II, Stewart was granted land in Badenoch, with its powerful castle of Lochindorb and became his father's lieutenant in the north. In 1382 his influence grew by marriage to the Countess of Ross and he was created Earl of Buchan. Alexander's rise was matched by a decline in the influence of the former regional superpower – the earldom of Moray. Unfortunately Stewart used his position to undermine central authority, to such a degree that, in 1388, he was dismissed from his position as justiciar – or chief law officer – north of the Forth as being "useless to the community".

When his brother succeeded as King Robert III, he proved incapable of checking Alexander's depredations. Bishop Bur of Moray had been paying the "Wolf" protection money but transferred his support to the House of Moray; he had also had the temerity to excommunicate Alexander for marital infidelity. The "Wolf" and his highland caterans responded by burning Forres in May 1390 and the rich and splendid cathedral of Elgin on 17 June 1390.

THE CONTEMPORARY VIEW

> . . . the ornament of the realm, the glory of the kingdom, the delight
> of foreigners and stranger guests. . .
>
> Bishop Bur to Robert III on Elgin Cathedral

THE WIDER VIEW

Stewart's outrages illuminate the problems of ruling what were two nations – a point the contemporary chronicler John of Fordun emphasised in his division of Scotland into the law-abiding inhabitants of the lowlands and the seaboard, and the Highlanders "wild and untamed. . . rough and unbending". The "Wolf" survived and prospered and is splendidly commemorated in Dunkeld Cathedral.

THE BATTLE OF HARLAW

Kings of Scots often had to watch as unruly subjects contested with each other for power. In this case the combatants were the Earl of Mar and Donald, Lord of the Isles. The cause of this bloody fracas, long remembered as "The Red Harlaw", was a dispute over the Earldom of Ross. The inconclusive battle was, however, followed by the withdrawal westward of the Islesmen. Mar and the burgesses of Aberdeen, who had come out in his support, claimed the victory.

The Oxford-educated Donald, was, like others of his line, defiant of central authority to the point of allying with the English, who however did nothing to help on this occasion as Donald and Red Hector of the Battles, the Maclean chief, led a host of ten thousand across Scotland. In a sense the repulse of the Islesmen and their Lord secured the "independence" of the mainland.

THE CONTEMPORARY VIEW

. . . the civilised Scots. . . did not put Donald to open rout, though they firecely strove, and not without success, to put a check to the audaciousness of the man

John Major, *History of Greater Britain (1521)*

O Children of Conn, remember
Hardihood in time of battle:
Be watchful, daring,
Be dextrous, winning renown
Be vigorous, pre-eminent,
Be strong, nursing your wrath. . .

From "Clan Donald's incitement to battle on the day of the Battle of Harlaw" by Lachlan Mor MacMhuirich.

THE WIDER VIEW

The "curse" of the Stewarts, long minorities of their kings, left Scotland prey to the great territorial magnates such as the Regent Albany, the King's uncle and ruler of Scotland for most of James's Ist's 18-year captivity, and the manipulating force behind the anarchic struggles of which Harlaw was an example.

THE FOUNDATION OF
ST ANDREWS UNIVERSITY

Throughout the Middle Ages various accounts of the Scots in Europe include tales of wanderings scholars at universities in France, Germany and Italy, and others on the teaching side, notably the great figure of Duns Scotus from Berwickshire. English universities too, regularly had Scots enrolled, despite the chilliness of Anglo-Scottish relations. John Balliol (the father of the King) "a lover of scholars, made, for the sake of God, a house perpetually endowed, at Oxford" and his widow, Devorguilla, founded the college which bears his name. Letters of safe conduct were issued to enable Scots students to continue their studies even in time of war.

During the Great Schism (1378-1418) the free movement of scholars was hampered – Scotland supporting the anti-Pope Benedict in Avignon – and a growing desire for learning led to Bishop Henry Wardlaw of St Andrews formally establishing Scotland's first university in 1412, although teaching had commenced in 1410.

THE CONTEMPORARY VIEW

We ordain that our scholars shall speak Latin in common. . . and if anyone. . . do not. . . he shall be separated from the common table to eat by himself, and shall be served last of all.

Devorguilla's Charter

We desire with all our might. . . that [the university] may rejoice in the fullness of its peaceful and prosperous estate, and that the study of divine and human laws of medicine, and of the liberal arts or faculties may be ardently carried on.

Bishop Wardlaw's Foundation

THE WIDER VIEW

The new university prospered and won approval, first from the schismatic Pope and then in 1418, on Scotland's return to the Roman fold the university led the arguments for rejecting Benedict and adhering to Pope Martin V – "Against him [a supporter of Benedict] rose up the whole University of St Andrews." *Scotichronicon*

JAMES I FREED AFTER 18 YEARS OF CAPTIVITY

King Robert III planned to send his 12-year-old heir, James, to France for safety. In March 1406 his ship was seized by English pirates and the boy handed over to Henry IV of England. Robert died in April, James succeeded and his uncle, the Duke of Albany *(q.v.)*, became Regent. James I spent 18 years as an English state prisoner and political pawn.

Henry V, at war with France, Scotland's ally, made James join his forces and at the seige of Melun, in 1420, used James's presence in the field to justify his execution of captured Scots in the French service as rebels against their lawful King.

One by-product of captivity was an excellent education – James became an accomplished poet – another was his wife, Joan Beaufort. Eventually, in April 1424, in exchange for £40,000, brazenly described as the fee for his board, James returned to Scotland to begin his personal rule, which ended with his murder in 1437.

THE CONTEMPORARY VIEW

If God grant me life and aid, even the life of a dog, throughout all the realm I will make the key keep the castle and the bracken bush the cow
James I quoted in Abbot Bower's *Scotichronicon*

THE WIDER VIEW

As this suggests, James gave priority to order and controlling the powerful nobles. His first-hand observation of the powerful English monarchy had given him ideas which were not always applicable to Scotland. He moved to destroy the power of his Albany relatives. His uncle had died in 1420, but Albany's son Murdoch had succeeded, with less competence, as Regent. Murdoch and various kinsmen were executed in 1425. James's authoritarian approach became seen as tyrannical and the support his law and order initiative might have generated was lost.

THE BLACK DINNER

Had the ancient tradition, or Law of Tanistry, of the Celtic kings still been in place, a suitable successor would have assumed the throne when James I was murdered in 1437. Instead, a six-year-old James II succeeded, ushering in a period of blood-boltered unrest involving a host of unruly subjects. Within 12 years three Earls of Douglas were dead; one, James the Gross, died in his bed, but the others were done to death in royal castles.

The young King, like so many of the Stewarts in their minorities, became the prize of a power struggle among the nobles, in this case Crichton and Livingston, contesting with the powerful House of Douglas. Crichton, as Regent, invited William, the sixth earl, a boy of 14, to Edinburgh Castle and, tradition has it, caused him and his younger brother to be killed before James. The melodramatic cue for the deed was, according to Boece, the placing of a bull's head on the table.

THE CONTEMPORARY VIEW

Edinburgh Castle, towne and tower,
God grant ye sink for sin!
And that for the black denner
Yerl Douglas gat therein
                    Old Ballad

THE WIDER VIEW

In 1449, James, now 19, was able to assume power for himself. The Douglas family continued to pose a threat and, in a savage echo of the earlier event, James stabbed to death the eighth earl, while he was under safe conduct in Stirling Castle. "The Earl was guilty of his own death by resisting the King's gentle persuasion", Parliament tactfully adjudged. With the advice and support of Bishop Kennedy of St Andrews, James then brought a measure of good government to Scotland until his premature death, killed by an exploding cannon at Roxburgh in 1460.

1472

THE ANNEXATION OF ORKNEY AND SHETLAND

A marriage treaty under which James III wed the daughter of Christian I of Denmark initiated a series of events which led to the annexation of Orkney and Shetland and ended six hundred years of Norse rule. Under the treaty, Christian pledged his lands and rights in the islands as part of the marriage dowry and, as the pledge was never redeemed, the rights passed to the Scottish crown which formally annexed the Earldom of Orkney and the Lordship of Shetland. At the same time there was a transfer of the bishopric of Orkney and Shetland from the jurisdiction of Trondheim in Norway to St Andrews, although social features like the unique systems of land tenure and the Norse tongue remained for many years.

THE CONTEMPORARY VIEW

James the thrid beand of the age of nynteine zeiris the counsall thocht it expedient that he sould haue ane wyff and for quhilk caus send ambassadouris. . . and. . . meid the contracttis between the twa kingis of mariage and that the king of Denmark and Norroway sould gif ovir all titill of richt that he had or micht haue vnto the landis of Orknay and Scheitland with vthir gret sowmes of money in name of touchar guide. . .
Lindesay of Pitscottie: *Historie and Cronicles of Scotland* (c.1575)

THE WIDER VIEW

The people of the islands would have cause to regret the passing of Norse government, as they suffered under Scots misrule, in particular the cruelties of the Stewart earls of Orkney. Nineteenth-century agricultural revolution brought prosperity and the islands' strategic importance, on the Norse sea-routes from Scandinavia to Britain and Iceland, returned with the two world wars. In the late twentieth century possession of the islands has greatly extended Britain's share of North Sea oil *(q.v.)*.

1493

THE FORFEITURE OF THE LORDSHIP OF THE ISLES

The semi-independent kingdom, embracing at its widest the Hebrides and almost the entire Western seaboard of Scotland together with Antrim, established by the heirs of Somerled *(q.v.)*, the Chiefs of MacDonald, had been a cultured state with a sophisticated court. The Lordship – the title was assumed in the fourteenth century – presented a challenge to the Scottish Kings; its rulers acknowledged only token allegiance to the Scottish crown and had thought little of establishing an independent foreign policy, creating alliances with Norway or England.

The vicissitudes of Scottish kingship provided an environment in which the MacDonald chiefs could preserve their independence. Their attempts to extend their influence, as for example in pursuit of the Earldom of Ross, had led to conflicts such as the Battle of Harlaw *(q.v.)*. The more effective Scottish kings attempted to control them – James I twice imprisoned Alexander the third Lord. The fourth and last Lord, John, demonstrates his house's tendencies; he had rebelled against James II in 1452 and in 1462 had signed the Treaty of Westminster-Ardtornish with Edward IV of England, agreeing the division of Scotland in the event of a successful English invasion, a clearly treasonable act against James III. His Lordship was, un-surprisingly, forfeited in 1475, but later restored. However James IV's Hebridean policy continued James I's work and he finally suppressed the Lordship in 1493.

THE CONTEMPORARY VIEW

. . . without them is no strength;
it is no joy without Clan Donald
    From "Giolla Colum mac an Ollaimh" in
        The Book of the Dean of Lismore

THE WIDER VIEW

The overthrow of MacDonald hegemony left a power vacuum in the West Highlands, one which was increasingly filled by the rise, from comparative obscurity, of the Campbells of Argyll, a clan increasingly identified with central authority.

THE FIRST WRITTEN REFERENCE TO SCOTCH WHISKY

In the Scottish Exchequer Roll for 1494 appears the entry "Delivery to Friar John Cor of eight bolls of malt to make *acqua vitae*". Assuredly this was not the first distilling of the water of life (uisge beatha in the Gaelic) – whisky – but it is apparently the first reference to it in official documents. Government has continued to take a lively interest in the product and in its revenue raising potential. In 1644 the Scots Parliament introduced an excise duty of 2/8d (13p) in the pint.

The first official record of a distillery appears in 1690, naming the Ferintosh distillery near Culloden. Ferintosh became synonymous with the best Highland malt whisky and was asked for by George IV on his visit to Scotland in 1822 (q.v.).

A new excise act in 1823 eliminated thousands of illicit stills in the Highlands and encouraged the development of legitimate commercial distilling, the first licence under the new Act being taken out by George Smith of Glenlivet in 1824. In 1830 the Coffey still made possible the mass-production of grain whisky as opposed to the pot still malt whisky, leading to the popularisation, at the end of the nineteenth century, of the proprietary blended whiskies.

THE CONTEMPORARY VIEW

FREEDOM *and* WHISKY *gang the thegither*
> Robert Burns: *The Author's Earnest Cry and Prayer. . .*
> (1784/85)

. . . Dr Johnson. . . called for a gill of whisky. "Come let me see what it is that makes a Scotchman happy!"
> James Boswell, *Journal of a Tour to the Hebrides* (1785)

THE WIDER VIEW

The Scotch Whisky industry now generates some £2,000,000,000 in foreign sales alone each year – a far cry from the 1400 bottles that the Inverness friar would have made from his eight bolls of malt.

THE MARRIAGE OF THE THISTLE AND THE ROSE

Was the end in sight for the age old enmity between Scotland and England when in 1503 King James IV of Scotland married Margaret Tudor, the eldest daughter of King Henry VII of England? James, an able and intelligent ruler alive to the new ideas of the Renaissance, had inherited the throne at the age of 15 after his father's murder in 1488. He was anxious to improve relationships with England and his marriage was part of a careful diplomatic offensive and brought with it a treaty of perpetual peace.

The 13-year-old Princess came north with a great entourage and reached Dalkeith, outside Edinburgh, on 3rd August. She stayed at the great Cistercian Abbey of Newbattle and was visited there by the 30-year-old James, before being married in the chapel of Holyrood Palace on 8th August.

Margaret was to bear three children who all died early in infancy before giving birth to the future James V in 1512.

THE CONTEMPORARY VIEW

Now fair, fairest of every fair,
Princess most pleasant and preclare,
The lustiest one alive that been,
Welcome of Scotland to be Queen

Welcome the Rose both red and white,
Welcome the flour of our delight!
Our secret rejoicing from the sun bien,
Welcome of Scotland to be Queen;
Welcome of Scotland to be Queen!
  William Dunbar (c.1460–c.1520)

THE WIDER VIEW

The Anglo-Scottish peace came under strain as James developed a French alliance and broke down with the war of 1513 and the Battle of Flodden *(q.v.)*. However, a century later James's policy triumphed in the Union of the Crowns of 1603 *(q.v.)*; his great-grandson James VI's accession to the throne of England by right of his descent from Margaret Tudor.

SCOTLAND'S FIRST PRINTING PRESS

On 15 September 1507 King James IV granted to Andrew Myllar, an Edinburgh bookseller and Walter Chepman, an Edinburgh merchant, the exclusive privilege of running a printing press. Myllar had studied printing in France and from there would import the necessary machinery and technicians to their Cowgate printing works. The introduction of printing was an important part of the King's cultural ambitions for his realm.

The new press's planned work included the production of a new Latin breviary but Chepman and Myllar also printed secular books and William Dunbar's poems were among the first works they produced in 1508.

Printing and publishing would become a major Scottish industry, a development accelerated by the Reformation emphasis on the availability of the Scriptures in the vernacular and the strong Scottish commitment to universal education. However the early years showed little evidence of this – the years from 1507 to 1600 saw only some 300 titles printed in Scotland. Chepman and Myllar's partnership did not last long and many of Scotland's leading writers continued to go abroad to have their work printed.

THE CONTEMPORARY VIEW

The Royal Patent described Chepman and Myllar's function as being:

> . . . for our plesour, the honour and profit of our realme and leigis, takin on thame to furnis and bring home ane prent, with all stuff belanganed tharto, and expert men to use the samyne for imprenting within our realme of the bukis of our lawis, actis of parliament, cronicles, mess bukis. . . and all utheris bookis that salbe seen necessaris and to sel the sammyn for competent pricis.

THE WIDER VIEW

Scotland was a comparatively late entrant to the printing revolution. Gutenberg had established his press in Mainz around 1450 and Caxton introduced printing into England in 1477.

THE LAUNCH OF THE
GREAT MICHAEL

King James IV's ambition for his realm at times over-reached itself, as in the case of the warship *Great Michael*. Launched from a specially constructed shipyard at Newhaven, near Edinburgh, this 240 foot long ship with a crew of 300 sailors and 120 gunners was incomparably larger than any other ship in the Scottish navy. Its construction taxed the resources of the nation and much of the specialised equipment and personnel had to be imported.

The building of *Great Michael* reportedly consumed all the wood of Fife, except that in the royal hunting grounds at Falkland. This may not, however, have amounted to a great deal of mature timber and additional supplies were imported from Norway. James's naval activity was extensive and his west coast base at Dumbarton was also an important centre of naval construction.

In the war of 1513 *(q.v.)*, she battered the English fortifications at Carrickfergus in Ulster, and was such a potent, if unwieldy weapon, that in the pre-war diplomatic skirmishings both France and England had sought to secure her services.

THE CONTEMPORARY VIEW

. . . the king of Scottland bigit ane great scheip callit the great Michell quhilk was the greattest scheip and maist of strength that ewer saillit in Ingland or France. . . Scho was so strang and wyde of length and breid that all the wryghtis of Scottland. . . and money other strangeris was at hir devyse. . .

Lindesay of Pitscottie, *Historie and Cronicles of Scoland* (c.1575)

THE WIDER VIEW

After Carrickfergus *Great Michael* sailed to France and was sold to Louis XII for 40,000 francs. Her new owners made little use of their acquisition and the vessel which the French king had thought the greatest ship in Christendom was allowed to rot away in Brest harbour.

THE COMPILATION OF THE
BOOK OF THE DEAN OF LISMORE

The island of Lismore, in the Sound of Kerrera, has an ecclesiastical history dating back to the Columban period, and its church of Kilmoluaig was briefly the Cathedral of the Diocese of Argyll. James MacGregor was appointed Dean of Lismore and a collection of Gaelic verse which he collected and transcribed between 1512 and 1542 is generally known as *The Book of the Dean of Lismore*.

Gaelic literature was essentially oral and a highly respected bardic caste existed whose role was the composition and transmission of poetry and song reflecting the accomplishments and traditions of the chiefly houses. One such bardic family were the MacMhuirichs, hereditary bards to the MacDonald Lords of the Isles.

MacGregor's collection includes work by the MacMhuirichs, by Irish bards, and work from a wide range of Scottish Gaelic sources as well as heroic ballads of the Ossianic legends. Although the probability of survival through the oral tradition was obviously higher in the case of the bardic praise poems and historical ballads, the collection also includes some more vernacular material – love songs, bawdry and satire.

THE CONTEMPORARY VIEW

Ní h-eibhnas gan Chlainn Domnhaill,
ní comhnairt bheith 'ne n-éagmhais;
an chlann dob fhearr san gcruinne:
gur dhiobh gach duine céatach.

It is no joy without Clan Donald,
it is no strength without them;
the best race in the round world:
to them belongs every goodly man.
    from "Giolla Colum mac an Ollaimh"
    in *The Book of the Dean of Lismore*

THE WIDER VIEW

MacGregor's collection, now preserved in the National Library of Scotland, provides one of the best sources of Gaelic poetry. Its rediscovery in the eighteenth century contributed to the revival of interest in Gaelic literature, a major manifestation of which was Macpherson's *Ossian (q.v.)*.

THE BATTLE OF FLODDEN

The Auld Alliance *(q.v.)*, had advantages but it drew Scotland into European conflicts of little national interest. The Holy League was formed in 1511 by the Papacy, Spain and Venice to limit French power in Italy. When England joined the League in 1513 France demanded Scotland's support which she provided by way of the *Great Michael (q.v.)* and by James IV agreeing to invade England.

His army was a national one, including a strong Highland contingent, a reflection of James's prestige and authority. It included 17 ox-drawn cannon although his best gunners were serving with the navy. The main English force was encountered on 9th September at Flodden. The English commander, the Earl of Surrey, outmanouevred James and was able to make better use of artillery, silencing the ill-sited Scottish cannon and forcing the King from the high ground. The Scots attacked in their traditional schiltron formation of pikemen, however the rough ground broke up the formations allowing the English to use their shorter halberds or bills effectively and win a hard-fought but decisive victory.

THE CONTEMPORARY VIEW

. . . the Master gonner of the Englishe parte slewe the Master gonner of Scotlande and bet all hys men from theyr ordinaunce, so that the Scottish ordinaunce did no harme to the Englishemen. . .
Hall, *Chronicle containing the History of England*

THE WIDER VIEW

Scottish casualties at Flodden were high both numerically and in the loss of the national leadership. James died gallantly, if needlessly, leaving his five month old son as heir. The consequences were significant both for the long and troubled minority of James V and a national loss of confidence and growing doubts about the Franco-Scottish alliance.

Flodden was perhaps the first European battle in which artillery played a decisive role.

THE DEATH OF GAVIN DOUGLAS

Scotland, in the years leading up to the Battle of Flodden *(q.v.)* saw a great flowering of literature. The Makars, a term embracing such disparate talents as Dunbar, Henryson and Gavin Douglas, were celebrated in William Dunbar's great mourning dirge, the "Lament for the Makaris":

"I se that makaris among the laif
Playis heir ther pageant, syne gois to graif;
Sparit is nocht ther faculte;
Timor mortis conturbat me".

Gavin Douglas (c.1474–1522) is one of the most distinguished of this group of poets. A younger son of Archibald Douglas, fifth Earl of Angus, he moved in court, church and intellectual circles, eventually becoming Bishop of Dunkeld in 1515.

His poetic fame chiefly rests on his translation of Virgil's *Aeneid* into Middle Scots, and in particular on his original prologues to each of the 13 books. These, especially the descriptions of the seasons, with their vitality and use of everyday language and imagery, gave a new force to the language.

THE CONTEMPORARY VIEW

The water-linnis routtis, and every lind
Whisslit and brayt of the swouchand wind.
Puir laboureris and busy husbandmen
Went wet and weary draglit in the fen;
The silly sheep and their little herd-groomis
Lurkis under lea of bankis, wodis, and broomis …

   Gavin Douglas, Prologue to Book VII of *The Eneados*

THE WIDER VIEW

Douglas's motivation was, in part at least, to use Virgil's masterpiece to give authority and status to the Scots language as a suitable vehicle for poetic expression. His *Eneados*, completed by 1513 and dedicated to Henry, Lord Sinclair, Captain of the *Great Michael (q.v.)* was, despite being, in Douglas's words, "in the langage of Scottis natioun", published in London in 1553, the first complete translation of Virgil's work.

THE FOUNDATION OF THE COURT OF SESSION

In the Middle Ages the rule of law in Scotland was enforced by a network of local courts – many landowners enjoyed the right of pit and gallows and the burghs also had courts. The King's justice was dispensed by royally appointed sheriffs and justiciars, though to add to confusion, some sheriffdoms were hereditary. From 1426 Parliament had held judicial sittings and there was a move towards the provision of a centralised system of justice through the King's Council and judicial committees of Parliament sitting in regular sessions in Edinburgh. Such courts were staffed by a mixture of clerical lawyers and unqualified laymen serving in the royal council or in Parliament.

In 1532, in the reign of James V, Parliament passed the College of Justice Act establishing a permanent court of 15 judges (8 were originally intended to be churchmen and 7 laymen) or "Lords of Council and Session" or "Senators of the College of Justice" as they were variously known. This created a central court for civil actions and the Court of Session has continued to exercise this role. Later developments established a supreme criminal court, utilising, in different robes, the judges of the Court of Session; the Lord President of the Court of Session becoming Lord Justice General when dispensing criminal justice in the High Court of Justiciary.

THE CONTEMPORARY VIEW

*Concerning the ordour of Justice and the institutioun of ane college
of cunning and wise men for the administratioun of Justice. . .
. . . to sitt and decyde apoun all actions civile*

From the College of Justice Act 1532

THE WIDER VIEW

The Court of Session was partly a pragmatic response to growing pressure on the King's Council, but it also represented another stage in the creation of a centralised modern bureaucratic state.

1540

THE FIRST PRODUCTION OF
ANE PLEASANT SATIRE OF THE THRIE ESTAITIS

When first presented before the court of James V at Linlithgow, Sir David Lyndsay's morality play created a sensation with its satirical view of the three estates of the realm, the lords Temporal and Spiritual and the Burgesses. None escaped, but of the three the clergy bore the brunt of Lyndsay's wit and mordant humour. All the more remarkable that the play enjoyed the special favour and patronage of the King, who was so taken with it that he threatened to "stick with the whinger [dagger]" some of the offending prelates. The King, of course, would appreciate that he was identified with the people – "Rex Humanitas".

Taking a whole day to perform in its lengthened form which was presented in public at Edinburgh and Cupar in the 1550s, the play seems to have endeared itself to the ordinary people who would appreciate the many broadly comic interludes. Lyndsay was himself, however, part of the court establishment, being Lord Lyon King of Arms.

THE CONTEMPORARY VIEW

Flatterie: *But I would have, ere we depairtit*
              A drink to mak us better heartit.

Deceit: *Weel said, by Him that herryit hell,*
              I was evan thinkan that mysel!

THE WIDER VIEW

This was a first flowering of a new kind of drama in Scottish soil, before any comparable piece in England. The "tragedy" is, however, that the theatre in Scotland would soon be blighted by the forces of the same reform of the church which Lyndsay was calling for and it would be many years before plays of any kind would be presented in this country. In the twentieth century, happily, Lyndsay's great achievement has enjoyed an astonishing revival of public esteem, including splendid performances in the home of the Kirk.

THE COMPLETION OF THE PALACE AT STIRLING CASTLE

James IV is usually seen as Scotland's pre-eminent Renaissance prince because of his enthusiasm for the arts and all forms of learning, but a good case can also be made for his son. *The Thrie Estaitis (q.v.)* was first produced in the reign of James V and at the Castle of Stirling he caused to be built a Renaissance-influenced Palace which introduced an architectural style which was virtually unknown anywhere else in Britain.

James was fond of Stirling; he roamed the area incognito as the "Gudeman of Ballengeich", and it was to Stirling he escaped in 1528 after being "coupit from hand to hand" during his minority. The stylistic influences of the Palace are plainly French and it is probable that the King's two marriages to French princesses had led to the introduction of skilled stoneworkers and artists.

THE CONTEMPORARY VIEW

Of the King's court at Stirling
> *Thou suld have heard the ornate Oratours,*
> *Makand his Hieness salutatioun,*
> *Baith of the Clergy, Toun and Counsalours,*
> *With many notable narratioun;*
> *Thou suld have seen his Coronatioun,*
> *In the fair Abbey of the Holy Rude,*
> *In presence of ane mirthful multitude*
> > Sir David Lyndsay: *The Deploratioun on the Deith of Queen Magdalene* (Queen Magdalene was James's first wife).

THE WIDER VIEW

The classical façade which faces the Lower Square of the Castle complex is probably the Palace's chief glory as we see it today, with its row of plain but graceful windows interspersed by the flourish of oval-headed niches with statues perched in them, The statues include classical gods, "Old Nick", and James himself. The detail of the Royal Chambers can only be imagined, but the wonderful carved wooden ceiling bosses or "Stirling Heads" are striking survivors.

THE ROUGH WOOING

"It cam with a lass and it will gang with a lass". With these reflections on the Stewart dynasty, the disheartened James V died in 1542, after the Scots defeat at the Battle of Solway Moss resisting the aggressive moves of Henry VIII. Anglo-Scottish relations entered a period of bitter hostility, which would continue until the young Mary, Queen of Scots was sent to France four years later.

Henry by this time had made his break with Rome and intended to force a Protestant Reformation on his northern neighbour – the Scots were divided, but the French party of the Queen Mother, Mary of Guise, gained the ascendancy and persuaded the Estates to repudiate English overtures for a marriage between the infant Queen and Prince Edward. Henry's response was to order Somerset to invade in 1544 and again in 1545, carrying out a savage war of attrition which left a folk-memory of hatred for the invaders in southern Scotland.

THE CONTEMPORARY VIEW

Put all to fyre and swoorde. . . burn Edinborough towne, so rased and defaced when ye have sacked and gotten what ye can of it, as there may remayne forever a perpetuel memory of the vengeance of God.
                              Edict of the English Privy Council

THE WIDER VIEW

There had been danger of war on another flank. The old English strategy of encouraging rebellion among the Islesmen raised a force of 8000 and 180 galleys, but quarrels hopelessly divided the Islesmen, "auld enemys to the realme of Scotland". Henry's death in 1547 offered only temporary respite – Protector Somerset resumed the "Rough Wooing" and inflicted a disastrous defeat at Pinkie. The English suit was only withdrawn when English armies were defeated in France and under the Treaty of Boulogne left Scotland in 1550.

1546

THE DEATH OF WISHART
AND BEATON

George Wishart was a preacher with unorthodox religious views who had found it wiser to live abroad for a while after the martyrdom of Patrick Hamilton in 1528. On the Continent he encountered fresh heresies, and, like his adherent John Knox *(q.v.)*, came to reject all beliefs unsupported by scriptural justification. Returning in 1543, his preaching attracted the unfavourable attention of Cardinal David Beaton, leader, with the Queen Mother, of the pro-French, anti-Protestant establishment. Wishart was arrested at Ormiston, East Lothian having sent Knox home with the words "Return to your bairns. . . One is sufficient for a sacrifice". Tried for heresy at St Andrews, he was burned there under the Cardinal's gaze on 1 March 1546. Beaton was assassinated two months later.

THE CONTEMPORARY VIEW

[The murder of Cardinal Beaton] *The said John Leslye. . . strook him anes or twice. . . But James Melven (a man of nature most gentill and most modest) perceiving thame both in choler, withdrew them, and said, "This work and judgement of God ought to be done with greater gravity," and presenting unto him the point of the sweard, said; "Repent thee of thy former wicked life, but especially of the schedding of the blood of that noble instrument of God, Maister George Wishart. . ." And so he stroke him twice or thrice through with a stog sweard*

John Knox, *History of the Reformation of Religion within the Realme of Scotland.*

THE WIDER VIEW

Beaton's assassination at his Castle of St Andrews by a group of Protestant lairds had as much to do with distaste for his pro-French policies as with religion. The flames of Wishart's martyrdom, however much it inspired Knox, did not spark off Reformation in Scotland, Protestantism remained a largely underground movement during most of the 1540s and 50s.

THE REFORMATION PARLIAMENT

Complex historical processes can seldom be given a single definitive date and the Reformation in Scotland is no exception. With Lutheran ideas current from 1525 and Tyndale's English New Testament circulating from 1530, a widespread internal reform movement had long been underway.

The Parliament, held in August 1560, however forms a convenient point of departure for the new Scottish, reformed Calvinist Church by giving legal force and public recognition to what was already a practical reality. Another indication of the way the wind was blowing was the Treaty of Edinburgh (July 1560), which ended the tradition of the "Auld Alliance" *(q.v.)* with France, saw French and English troops withdrawn from Scotland and France recognising Elizabeth Tudor as Queen of England.

The Reformation Parliament, meeting in the absence of any royal authority, the Regent Mary of Guise having died in June and Queen Mary still in France, passed measures abolishing the Latin Mass and denying Papal jurisdiction. More positively it endorsed the Confession of Faith as the foundation document of the new Church.

THE CONTEMPORARY VIEW

The three estatis. . . hes statute and ordainit that the bischope of Rome haif no jurisdictioun nor autoritie within this realme in tymes cuming. . .
Acts of the Parliament of Scotland

THE WIDER VIEW

The formalising of the Reformation in the 1560 Parliament owes as much to politics as it does to theology. The Lords of the Congregation, an alliance of peers and lairds, who were at the centre of the revolution – because it was little else – of 1559/60 were as concerned with international power politics as they were with doctrinal concerns. France, the old Catholic ally, had proved to have little to offer Scotland; Protestant England began to seem a more attractive and natural connection.

1566

THE MURDER OF RICCIO

Mary Stewart, Queen of Scots, had returned to her kingdom from France only five years previously – although a Catholic, her desire not to intentionally offend the Reformers was made clear from the outset. In July 1565 she made her first serious misjudgement. She impulsively married her unimpressive half-cousin Henry Stewart, Lord Darnley, and Darnley was a Catholic. So for the first time there were grounds for suspicions of a religious nature; they were soon to be followed by rumours about the Queen's lifestyle.

Before they had been married a year, Darnley became the recipient or possibly the author of scurrilous tales about Mary and her charming Italian secretary, David Riccio. On 9 March 1566, a number of the nobility seized Riccio from her presence and stabbed him to death before the gaze of Darnley. The evidence shows Riccio to have been, in fact, a perfectly innocent courtier who was cultivated by the Queen because his musical talents were sympathetic to her own aesthetic disposition.

THE CONTEMPORARY VIEW

David Ricio. . . was a merry fallow, and a good mucitien, and her Maieste. . . wanted a bass to sing the fourt part.

Andrew Melville

THE WIDER VIEW

Mary was distressed, perhaps even unbalanced by this violent act – she was six months pregnant at the time – and it may have been the motive force behind her increasingly irrational actions over the next year. Her involvement with Darnley's assassination at Kirk o' Field in February 1567 was suspected, as was that of the Protestant Earl of Bothwell, and when she married Bothwell eight weeks later the other Protestant Lords moved against her. At Carberry Hill, on 15 June, she was taken from her forces and a month later forced to abdicate in favour of the infant James VI. Mary was executed in 1587 after a 20 year captivity.

THE DEATH OF ROBERT CARVER

The reign of James IV *(q.v.)*, as we know from Pedro de Ayala, the Spanish Ambassador, was a stage for the flowering of the Renaissance arts. This was the time of Henryson's *Testament of Cresseid*, of Gavin Douglas's translation of the *Aeneid*, and for the King's court itself, William Dunbar wrote *The Thistle and the Rose* to celebrate the marriage of James and Margaret Tudor *(q.v.)*. Also in and around the court of the music-loving, lute-playing king is the shadowy figure of Robert Carver, whom musicologists now identify as probably Scotland's greatest ever composer.

Carver, born around 1484, was trained in the "sang school" at Scone Abbey; his astonishing series of masses, plainsong and motets are only now, after five hundred years, again receiving the praise that they had during his lifetime.

THE CONTEMPORARY VIEW

January 1st 1506. Item, that day giffin to divers menstrales,
schawmeris, trumpetis, taubroneris, fithelars, lutaris, harparis, clarscharis,
piparis, extending to sixty-nine persons, ten pounds and eleven shillings.
Accounts of James IV

Schir, ye have mony servitouris
And officiaris of dyvers curis;
Kirkmen, courtmen and craftismen fyne
Doctouris in jure, and medicyne. . .
Musicianis, menstralis, and mirrie singaris:
Chevalouris, cawandaris and flingaris. . ."
William Dunbar, *Remonstrance to the King*

THE WIDER VIEW

Although details of Carver's life are extremely sketchy, it has been possible to establish links between his compositions and contemporary events. The motet called *O Bone Jesu* is believed linked with James IV's guilt over his involvement in his father's murder at Sauchieburn – "ever sade and dollorous in his mynd for the deid of his father". Later, as the reformation neared, Carver produced simpler settings of the Mass, perhaps indicating awareness of the way the wind was blowing, or responding to contemporary Catholic reform movements.

THE DEATH OF GEORGE BUCHANAN

A scholar, playwright, poet and political writer known and respected throughout Europe, Buchanan is now almost forgotten except as tutor to Mary, Queen of Scots, and the young James VI. His immense reputation in the intellectual circles of France, Portugal and England was gained through his skills as a Latinist and the purity of his style seems to have attracted the kind of admiration that enabled Dryden to judge him "comparable with any of the moderns and excelled by few of the ancients".

Born in 1506, the son of a laird at Killearn, he was educated first at the local school and at Dumbarton Academy, then at the universities of St Andrews and Paris, in both of which he was instructed by the Scots scholar John Major or Mair. On his return to Scotland in the 1560s he threw his intellectual powers on the Protestant side from his position as Principal of St Leonard's College, St Andrews. Appointed as James's tutor in 1570, Buchanan seems to have been the quintessential domineering schoolmaster, who beat his royal pupil regularly.

THE CONTEMPORARY VIEW

All the world knows that my master George Buchanan was a great master in that faculty. I follow his pronunciation both of his Latin and Greek, and am sorry that my people of England do not the like; for certainly their pronunciation utterly fails the grace of these two learned languages.

James VI, in a speech to Edinburgh University

THE WIDER VIEW

Buchanan's political tracts had only a limited impact, even on the pupil who grew up to rule two kingdoms. Perhaps all that James learned from his dominie was his pedantry. His role in providing an intellectual framework for the Scots Reformation is, however, not without significance.

SCOTLAND CELEBRATES NEW YEAR'S DAY ON JANUARY 1

Hogmanay and New Year's Day are so closely associated with Scottish tradition that it comes as a shock to realise that before 1600 the New Year officially started on March 25 (Lady Day). In December 1599 the King and his Privy Council resolved to bring Scotland into line with other countries.

THE CONTEMPORARY VIEW

The Kingis Majestie and Lordis of his Secreit Counsall undirstanding that in all utheris weill governit commoun welthis and cuntreyis the first day of the yeir begynis yeirlie upoun the first day of Januare, commounlie callit new yeiris day, and that this realme onlie is different fra all utheris in the compt and reckning of the yeiris. . . his Majestie with the advise of the Lordis of his Secreit Counsall statutis and ordanis that in all tyme cuming the first day of the yeir sal begin yeirlie upoun the first day of Januare. . .

Register of the Privy Council, 17 December 1599

THE WIDER VIEW

This Privy Council decision is significant, both for its immediate objective and as evidence of James VI's international outlook. The change reflected the adoption of the Gregorian calendar by European states in the 1580s. England did not change the start of the official legal year to January 1 until 1752. The measure also reflects his interest in government; James was the first Scottish ruler to write about the art of kingship. His *Basilikon Doron* published in 1599 and addressed to his son and heir, Prince Henry, contained the King's views on the art of good government. James's long reign saw the growing professionalisation and laicisation of administration. The Privy Council was a powerful legislative and administrative body, useful to the King because it was more easily influenced or controlled than his sometimes difficult Parliament.

THE UNION OF THE CROWNS

When Queen Elizabeth died in March 1603 James VI, King of Scots, peacefully inherited the English Crown. Elizabeth's aunt, Margaret Tudor, had married James's great-grandfather in 1503 *(q.v.)* and James was the legitimate and Protestant descendant of Henry VII and had been named, eventually, by Elizabeth as her heir. Centuries of conflict and warfare between the kingdoms had apparently ended in unity.

The accession of James to the English throne did not necessarily mean that the two states would become one – this was merely a Regnal Union. However James's views were clear enough – his post 1603 Scottish currency bore the motto *Quae Deus Coniunxit Nemo Separet* (What God has joined let no man separate); while his English coins read *Henricus rosas regna Jacobus* (Henry [VII united] the Roses, James [united] the kingdoms). One of his first acts was to ask, unavailingly, his two Parliaments to consider an incorporating Union. He repeatedly argued the case for union:

THE CONTEMPORARY VIEW

I desire a perfect Union of Lawes and persons, and such a Naturalizing as may make one body of both Kingdomes under mee your King. . . for no more possible is it for one King to governe two Countreys Contiguous, the one a great, the other a less, a richer and a poorer. . . than for one head to governe two bodies. . .

King James VI & I (1607)

This disparity was indeed the difficulty. James's first action, on being advised that the English crown was his, was to borrow 10,000 merks from the city of Edinburgh to meet the cost of his progress to London. Scotland was a smaller and poorer land, a land of unruly magnates, a land which had but a conditional respect for kingship. James's title was King of Scots, not of Scotland. Majesty, stability and wealth awaited him in London and he soon learned to enjoy living and reigning in the English style. His promises to return to Scotland every three years never materialised – one visit north, in 1617, was all he managed in the 22 years of his dual monarchy.

In her King's absence Scotland still needed to be governed and James, though 400 miles away, took a lively interest in Scottish affairs, corresponding frequently with his Council in Scotland. James had been an active and forceful King in Scotland and had done much to stabilise the country, especially those troubled areas of the Highlands and the Borders. With access to the more evolved English administrative structures his rule over Scotland continued to be skilful, not least because of his personal knowledge and experience, an asset his son Charles would not enjoy.

THE CONTEMPORARY VIEW

Here I sit and govern with my Pen, I write and it is done, and by a Clearke of the Councill I governe Scotland now, which others could not doe by the sword.

James VI & I – speech to English Parliament. 1607.

THE WIDER VIEW

James led his Court south with a dream of a true incorporating union. His new subjects willingly accepted a Scottish Protestant King, anything was better than religious or civil wars; but they were reluctant to let Scots share in trade or the spoils of office. The removal of the Court economically impoverished Scotland and left a gap in her politics and culture with London becoming the focus for ambition. Even in Scotland English rather than Scots became increasingly the language of scholarship and literature, a process greatly hastened by one of the scholar-King's favourite projects – the 1611 Authorised Version of the Bible.

1614

NAPIER PUBLISHES HIS TABLES OF LOGARITHMS

John Napier, laird of Merchiston Castle on the outskirts of Edinburgh, was a complex character, a devout Presbyterian and commentator on the Book of Revelations who equally enthusiastically believed in astrology. He suggested the construction of a giant burning glass to destroy the Turkish army and, Leonardo-like, conceived of the tank: "a round chariot of mettle made of the proof of double muskett. . ." Born in 1550 and educated at St Andrews, he travelled widely on the continent before producing his most famous work *Mirifici Logarithmorum Canonis Descriptio*. This gave to the world an entirely new way of calculating – logarithmic tables, which greatly facilitated complex mathematical calculations.

Napier's work was instantly recognised by the international scientific community for its originality and importance. Johann Kepler, the great German mathematician and astronomer, praised his achivement and dedicated a book to him.

THE CONTEMPORARY VIEW

Seeing there is nothing (right well beloved students of Mathematics) nor is so troublesome to mathematical practice, that doth molest and hinder calculations more than the multiplications, divisions, square and cubical extractions of great numbers, which besides the tedious expense of time are for the most part subject to many slipping errors, I began to therefore to consider in my mind by what certain and ready art I might remove these hindrances.

Napier's Introduction to *The Admirable Canon of Logarithms*

THE WIDER VIEW

Until the advent of the electronic calculator and the computer logarithmic tables and the slide rule developed from them were the only means of speeding up complex mathematical calculations. Napier's invention, though later superseded by other tables, made more practicable the mathematically-dependent scientific and engineering developments which followed. It is not too much to place Napier in the first rank of mathematicians alongside Isaac Newton.

A SCHOOL IN EVERY PARISH

In 1496 James IV's parliament, to ensure good governance by an educated elite, ordered all barons and freeholders of substance to send their heirs to school and then to college.

In 1560 Knox and his fellow Reformers' *First Book of Discipline*, mindful that the "Church here in earth shall be taught not by angels but by men", planned the "virtuous education and godly upringing of the youth of the realm". A three-layered provision of universal education was envisaged, with elementary schools in each parish, grammar schools in the burghs and a college in each principal town. Education was to be funded through the church, but the appropriation of church property by lay proprietors and the post-Reformation turmoil frustrated the accomplishment of Knox's visionary plan.

In 1616 the Privy Council ordered the establishment of an English school in every parish to promote learning and "trew religioun" and eradicate the Gaelic language, an instruction Parliament confirmed in 1633.

THE CONTEMPORARY VIEW

...that all his Majesties subjectis, especiallie the youth, be exercised and trayned up in civilitie, godlines, knawledge, and learning, that the vulgar Inglishe toung be universallie plantit, and the Irishe language, whilk is one of the cheif and principall causis of the continewance of barbaritie and incivilitie amongis the inhabitantis of the Ilis and Heylandis, may be abolisheit and removit. . . in everie parroche of the kingdome. . . a scoole salbe establisheit and a fitt persone appointit to teache the same. . .

Act of the Privy Council, 10 December 1616

THE WIDER VIEW

State education, however imperfectly implemented, had significant results. Mass literacy was achieved, in the Lowlands at least, by the eighteenth century – for proof see the miners' libraries at Leadhills and Wanlockhead *(q.v.)* and the literate environment which bred poets like Burns and Fergusson.

THE FIVE ARTICLES OF PERTH

James VI was anxious to integrate and unify his kingdoms and religious policy was an important element in this. In London he had embraced the English prayer book and on his visit to Scotland in 1617 used the English forms in his private chapel. At the 1617 General Assembly James proposed reforms to bring the Scottish church in line with England – this failed but at Perth in 1618 the so-called Five Articles were pushed through by a two to one majority. The articles dealt with the observance of the main dates in the Christian calendar, lay confirmation by bishops, private Communion and private baptism in case of infirmity, and, most controversially, because most public, the requirement to take Communion kneeling. This last mainly affected the laity and its echoes of the observance of the Mass proved a particular source of contention.

THE CONTEMPORARY VIEW

Forsameikle as in the Generall Assemblie of the Kirk, holden latlie at our Burgh of Perth. . . there were certane godlie and good acts made and sett doun, concerning the glorie of God and governement of his church, agreeable to that decent and comlie order which was observed in the primitive kirk, when the same was in the greatest puritie and perfection. . . [Those not observing the Articles]. . . *sall be repute, holden, and esteemed as seditious, factious and unquyett persons. . .*
Privy Council ratification of the Five Articles, 1618

THE WIDER VIEW

The substantial public opposition to the Five Articles, despite the King's declared wishes to see them enacted, was significant and reveals the first signs of a rift between King and people over Church policy – a rift which would widen, under Charles I *(q.v.)* into open revolt. The post National Covenant *(q.v.)* General Assembly in 1638 repealed the Articles.

THE ESTABLISHMENT OF THE SCOTS COLONIES IN NOVA SCOTIA

In 1621, Sir William Alexander of Menstrie, poet, courtier and statesman, was granted by James VI & I a charter to settle large areas of Canada, known as New Scotland or Nova Scotia. In 1625, on the accession of Charles I, this charter was renewed and extended, effectively putting huge tracts of North America under Alexander's control.

A new Scottish Order of Baronets of Nova Scotia was established in 1625, the members being obliged to provide men for the new colony, an obligation later commuted to cash by a perennially impecunious monarchy.

Pioneers went out in 1622 and 1623, but the first settlement was not established until 1629. At first the settlement prospered but by 1632 the revival of French power in Canada forced the abandonment of the Scots colonies.

THE CONTEMPORARY VIEW

Charles I's Charter granted Alexander powers to use: *the mines and forests, erect cities, appoint fairs, hold courts, grant lands and coin money.*

THE WIDER VIEW

The settlement of Nova Scotia was largely modelled on James VI's Plantation of Ulster, another scheme accompanied by the creation of baronetcies to fund and furnish the new colony. The Ulster plantation attracted many lowland Scottish settlers on the forfeited estates of the Earls of Tyrone and Tyrconnel. By the middle of the century there were as many as 50,000 Scots settled in Ulster.

Nova Scotia attracted Highland Scottish settlement in the later eighteenth century and areas of the province today still maintain a Gaelic culture.

In 1630 Alexander was created Viscount Stirling. In 1632 he built a fine Renaissance mansion in Stirling, still extant and now known as Argyle's Ludging. In 1633 he was advanced to the rank of Earl and given the appropriate additional title of Viscount Canada.

THE CORONATION OF
CHARLES I AT ST GILES

Charles's Coronation was a clumsy attempt to win popularity in his native Scotland which he had not visited since infancy. The Anglican rites in the ceremony held in St Giles, designated a Cathedral by Charles, revealed it as part of his strategy to impose alien forms of ecclesiastical government and ritual upon Scotland.

Charles had inherited James VI's belief in the divine nature of kingship but combined this with inept management of his ambitious programme which included a determination to enforce uniform episcopacy across his three kingdoms, and a failure to see the signs of resistance which would eventually lose him both crown and life.

The coronation did not end Charles's ineptitudes. Archbishop William Laud had by 1637 produced a *Revised Prayer Book* for Scotland, which provoked a fresh wave of protest because of its challenge to presbyterian belief in the necessity for "extempore" or spontaneous prayer. The riot at St Giles on the first reading of "Laud's Liturgy" sparked off further disorders involving the notorious Edinburgh mob.

THE CONTEMPORARY VIEW

Dost thou say Mass in my lug?

(Traditionally attributed to Jenny Geddes at the first reading from the Prayer Book)

Something similar probably was shouted, and even a cutty stool thrown, from the mob which played a large part in Edinburgh life. Had the ordinary Edinburgh people been present at the coronation their sentiments would probably have been very similar.

THE WIDER VIEW

Historians have suggested that Charles often simply followed policies laid down by his father. However he contributed to his own downfall by his insensitivity and marked capacity to alienate a wider range of people and interests as well as by being seen as the absentee monarch attempting to juggle the policies of three kingdoms.

THE SIGNING OF THE NATIONAL COVENANT

Signing began in Edinburgh's Greyfriars Kirkyard on 28 February. One author of this great petition against Charles I's unpopular religious and political policies, Archibald Johnston of Wariston, called it "The Great Marriage Day of this Nation with God", expressing the idea of Scotland entering a specially covenanted relationship with God. Popular enthusiasm swept the Lowlands as copies of the Covenant gathered thousands of signatures and an unusual degree of national unity seemed attainable – the first signature on the Covenant was that of the future Marquis of Montrose – and many of the nobility and gentry were, for the moment, allied with the "elect of God" and ministers, such as Covenant co-author, Alexander Henderson of Leuchars.

The Covenant's text was less revolutionary than the sentiments of the signatories and the atmosphere of the time.

THE CONTEMPORARY VIEW

. . . every one of us underwritten, Protest, that after. . . examination of our owne consciences, in matters of true and false Religion, we are now thoroughly resolved on the Truth, by the Word and Spirit of God. . . we abhorre and detest all contrary Religion and Doctrine. . . even as they are now damned and confuted by the word of God, and Kirk of Scotland.

The National Covenant

THE WIDER VIEW

The Covenant avoided the language of outright revolt, professing loyalty to the Crown, but started a train of events in which radical elements increasingly came out against Charles's government. There was open confrontation with the King's Commissioner, the Duke of Hamilton, at the Glasgow General Assembly of November 1638. Revolution was in the air. In an atmosphere which anticipated the French Convention or the Petrograd soviet, the Assembly deposed the bishops and the Prayer Book was condemned as being "heathenish, Popish, Jewish and Arminian". Civil war was now likely.

1643

THE SOLEMN LEAGUE AND COVENANT

Flushed with their success in the Bishop's Wars over a chastened Charles I, the ruling Covenanting party in Scotland were in a strong position to listen to the blandishments of both Royalists and Parliamentarians when the English Civil War began in 1642. Scotland's army under Leslie was an important factor when the Parliamentarians agreed to the Scots' terms in this pact, which, as the title suggests, was both military and religious. The terms were exacting in that the English side agreed to follow "the example of the best reformed churches", which the Scots believed meant that they would adopt the Scottish system of Presbyterianism. England would, in return, pay for the Scots to send south a substantial force of 20,000 men.

Part of the bargain was met the following year when the Scots army made a significant contribution to the defeat of the Royalists at Marston Moor; the religious implications of the League were not to be so easily delivered.

THE CONTEMPORARY VIEW

The English were for a civil League; we for a religious Covenant.
Rev. Robert Baillie (1602-1662)

THE WIDER VIEW

Among the English allies there had been, from the outset, a group of Independents in religion who had been unhappy about the ecclesiastical clauses imposing Presbyterianism. With the rise of Cromwell and the forging of his military machine, the need for the increasingly strident Presbyterian Scots was less apparent – ultimately, in fact, the machine was turned against them. The League's inherently logical aim of protecting the Scottish revolution by allying with the English against the King ultimately failed.

Not all of the Covenanters were content with the anti-royalist flavour of the League and there were those, like Montrose, who were to take a very different course.

THE BATTLE OF INVERLOCHY

On 2 February 1645 below a snow-covered Ben Nevis, James Graham, Marquis of Montrose routed the Covenanting forces of Archibald Campbell, Marquis of Argyll. Montrose, the first signatory of the National Covenant *(q.v.)*, but unwilling to make war on his King, now opposed his former allies. Montrose's tactics gained him a place in military history. Trapped with his small force of clansmen and Irish between two advancing forces, Montrose made a forced march up out of the Great Glen, into the winter mountains, outflanking Argyll's Campbells. The shock of the Highland charge was unstoppable; the slaughter of the Covenanting army was soon complete.

THE CONTEMPORARY VIEW

He either fears his fate too much
Or his deserts are small
That dare not put it to the touch
To win or lose it all

Montrose

Destruction take you if I pity your condition
as I listen to the misery of your children,
lamenting the mob who were in the battle,
the howling of the women of Argyll.

Ian Lom, "A song on the day
of the Battle of Inverlochy"

THE WIDER VIEW

Inverlochy started Montrose's *annus mirabilis*. After victories at Auldearn and Alford, Montrose routed a Covenanting army at Kilsyth and seemed able to hold Scotland for Charles I. By autumn the campaign lay in ruins; squabbling among his forces and indecision delayed plans to march south to aid the King. At Philiphaugh near Selkirk he was defeated by a larger army under David Leslie. Montrose escaped to France. In 1650, after Charles's execution, he made an ill-starred attempt to raise support for Charles II. The campaign was over before it began. Defeated at Carbisdale on the Dornoch Firth, Montrose was taken to Edinburgh and after a show trial was executed at the Mercat Cross in the High Street.

THE BATTLE OF DUNBAR

Charles I's execution produced an unexpected division between the Scots, among whom the clerical party predominated, and the English Parliamentarians under Oliver Cromwell. Scotland proclaimed Charles II king, having obtained his promise, in the Declaration of Breda, to adhere to the Solemn League and Covenant *(q.v.)*. When Charles landed at Garmouth, Cromwell's response was decisive. He crossed the Border and at first tried to reason with the General Assembly – "I beseech you in the bowels of Christ, think it possible you may be mistaken". This appeal was rejected and at Dunbar on 3 September Cromwell announced – "The Lord hath delivered them into our hands", when he saw that the Scots under David Leslie had left a strong hill-top position, probably under clerical pressure to mount an attack on the English. With supreme generalship, Cromwell broke through the right of the larger Scots army and then "rolled up" the whole line, killing 3,000 and taking 10,000 prisoners.

THE CONTEMPORARY VIEW

K. Charles behedit at Whytehall gate, in England, by that traiterous parliament and armey . . . one Tuesday the 30 of Januarij, 1649. . . Prince Charles proclaimed King of Grate Britane, France and Irland, at Edinburghe cross. . .

Lyon King of Arms

The Lord Hath delivered Antichrist into our hands and like Gideon you should descend on them and sweep them away before you.

Scottish clergy to Leslie on the
morning of the Battle of Dunbar

THE WIDER VIEW

This was not quite the end of Royalist resistance. The Scots collected a fresh army and Charles made a thrust into England, but the following year Cromwell won his "crowning mercy" at Worcester. Two days previously General Monck had sacked Dundee – Scotland's Drogheda. The Cromwellian Union, a union imposed by force of arms, followed soon after.

PENTLAND RISING

Charles II's restoration in 1661 re-established the episcopal system of church government and revived many royal prerogatives. There was considerable opposition in Scotland to the Restoration Settlement, particularly in the pro-Covenant south-west where both dissident clergy – the "outed" ministers who had lost their positions – and lay people widely disobeyed the laws and held outdoor services or conventicles.

To disperse these gatherings and collect fines for non-attendance at episcopal services, troops were sent into disaffected areas. In November 1666 the capture of Sir James Turner, commanding these forces, acted as the spark for an uprising. The revolt was not supported by the landowning classes who had backed the National Covenant of 1638. An ill-equipped and ill-led Covenant force of around 1000 marched on Edinburgh but was crushed on 28 November by stronger Government forces under General Tam Dalyell at Rullion Green in the Pentlands. Fifty were killed, 36 captured Covenanters were executed, others were transported to the plantations of Barbados and Virginia.

THE CONTEMPORARY VIEW

Farewell, sun, moon and stars. Farewell, kindred and friends, farewell, world and time, farewell, weak and frail body. Welcome eternity, welcome angels and saints.
Dying words of Hugh McKail, captured and tortured
after the Battle of Rullion Green.

THE WIDER VIEW

The Pentland Rising was perhaps Scotland's first popular insurrection and, as such, particularly alarming to authority. After the immediate period of repression a more moderate policy towards the Covenanters was introduced by the Duke of Lauderdale, although tension and repression increased in the "killing times" of the 1680s. The Covenanters are often represented as both religious martyrs and early fighters for civil liberty; however freedom of opinion was not a high priority and their determination to impose their own system of church government was absolute.

THE BATTLE OF BOTHWELL BRIDGE

The struggle over religious policy flared up in 1678. The billeting of troops – the so-called "Highland Host" – in disaffected areas of south-west Scotland, although short-lived, had exacerbated Covenanting sentiment. Conventicles continued to attract crowds of up to 14,000 and by 1679 many spoke of rebellion. Archbishop Sharp's murder by Covenanting extremists on 3 May and the Covenanter victory over Claverhouse at Drumclog, Lanarkshire, on 1 June, both served to mobilise support.

A Covenanting army, large in numbers, though fatally divided in policy, aims and leadership, mustered at Bothwell Bridge near Hamilton and on 22 June confronted a government force under the Duke of Monmouth, Charles II's illegitimate son. Monmouth's force won an easy victory with around 600 Covenanting casualties and 1200 prisoners taken.

THE CONTEMPORARY VIEW

. . . I had a wife and five children, and. . . a little bit of an estate, and that I was come to hazard all and my life; to get the yoke of prelacy and supremacy removed; but. . . they intended to tyrannize over our consciences; and lead us to a worse snare nor we were into. . .

James Ure of Shargarton

Ure fought at Bothwell Bridge but as the passage shows criticised the extreme Covenanting group led by Robert Hamilton and Richard Cameron for their rejection of any idea of freedom of conscience.

THE WIDER VIEW

Bothwell Bridge and Monmouth's political skill in dealing leniently with the aftermath effectively ended armed resistance. The followers of Richard Cameron remained unreconciled and in the 1680 "Sanquhar Declaration" declared war on Charles II. These "Cameronians" were the main target of the "Killing Times" of 1680-85. Despite Covenanting legend, only about 100 died in this period and the circumstances that brought them to execution were as much political as religious.

THE PUBLICATION OF THE
INSTITUTIONS OF THE LAW OF SCOTLAND

James Dalrymple of Stair (1619-1695) was appointed to the Court of Session under Cromwell but continued in office under Charles II, becoming successively a knight, a baronet, Lord President of the Court of Session in 1671 and was created Viscount of Stair in 1690 under William and Mary. Very much a political lawyer, he served in parliament between 1672 and 1681 but his claim to fame is his great work on the laws of Scotland, commonly known as Stair's *Institutions*.

The special character of Scots Law, its sources in Roman Law, French and Dutch practice and ethics was precious to Stair and his text eloquently defines and promotes the merits of the Scottish system. It still remains one of the pillars of Scots law.

THE CONTEMPORARY VIEW

There is not much here asserted on mere authority. . . but the rational motives, inductive of the several laws and customs, are therewith held forth:. . .

. . . the law of this kingdom hath attained to so great perfection, that it may, without arrogance, be compared with the laws of any of our neighbouring nations.

. . . we do always prefer the sense, to the subtilty, of law, and do seldom trip by niceties or formalities.

From Stair's "Dedication to the King" in the First Edition

THE WIDER VIEW

The publication of a law-book may seem an unlikely candidate for a significant Scottish date. However it can be fairly claimed for the *Institutions* that it did more than anything else to ensure the survival of a separate Scottish legal system at and after the Union of the Parliaments in 1707 *(q.v.)*. The *Institutions* established Scots law as an intellectually coherent entity, strong and adaptable enough to resist erosion from the English common law which would dominate the new United Kingdom.

THE BATTLE OF KILLIECRANKIE

William of Orange landed at Torbay in November 1688 and was formally offered the English crown on 13 February 1689, a month before the Convention of Estates met to declare the Scottish throne vacant. It was offered to William and Mary subject to acceptance of the Claim of Rights and the Articles of Grievances; documents concerning the independence of the Scottish Parliament and the establishment of presbyterianism.

John Graham of Claverhouse, Viscount Dundee, who had been active against the Covenanters during the Killing Times raised the standard of the exiled James VII & II on Dundee Law in April 1689. He gathered support from among the Catholic Highland Clans and after some skirmishing defeated a superior Government force under Mackay in the Pass of Killiecrankie near Pitlochry on 27 July. The traditional élan of the Highland charge won the day but Dundee was killed and with him died the prospects of Jacobite* success.

THE CONTEMPORARY VIEW

I faught at land, I faught at sea,
At hame I faught my auntie-o;
But I met the devil and Dundee
On the braes o' Killiecrankie-o.
                    Old Ballad

THE WIDER VIEW

Few historical figures have evoked such varied reactions as Graham of Claverhouse, the hate-figure "Bloody Clavers" to the Covenanters, "Bonnie Dundee" to the Jacobites and to poets like Scott:

To the Lords of Convention 'twas Claver'se who spoke,
'Ere the King's crown shall fall there are crowns to be broke;
So let each Cavalier who loves honour and me,
Come follow the bonnet of Bonny Dundee'.

Dundee's was the first in a line of Jacobite risings which ended with the crushing of the clans at Culloden *(q.v.)*.

---

*Jacobites were so named from "Jacobus" the Latin form of the name of the exiled King James.

THE PUBLICATION OF THE FIRST GAELIC BIBLE

An important tenet of the Reformers had been the availability of Scripture in the vernacular. However from an early date, Bibles in English, rather than Scots, were the norm in Scotland, with Tyndale's and Coverdale's versions being popular before the arrival, after 1611, of the King James or Authorised Version.

If Scots speakers were ill-served, then Gaelic speakers were even more disadvantaged, with no printed version of Scripture available to them until 200 copies of the "Bedell Bible", translated into Irish Gaelic and printed in Irish characters, were circulated in 1685. This was of only limited value and Robert Kirk, the Minister of Aberfoyle, transliterated the Old and New Testaments into Roman characters between 1688 and 1689, travelling to London in the spring of 1690 to see his work through the press.

THE CONTEMPORARY VIEW

Hic sepultus ille evangeli promulgator accuratus et linguae Hiberniae lumen. M. Robertus Kirk, Aberfoile Pastor. Obit 14 Maii 1692. Aetat 48

Kirk's tombstone in Aberfoyle

THE WIDER VIEW

The ubiquity of the Bible in English did much to undermine Scots as a literary language, a process aided by the removal of the Court to London in 1603 after the Union *(q.v.)*.

Robert Kirk, besides his fame as a translator of the Bible, wrote one of the more curious works of the seventeenth century – *The Secret Commonwealth*, a comprehensive guide to fairies, elves, brownies and all the rest of the "Subterranean (and for the most part) Invisible People". For his presumptuous interference in such mysteries, local folklore claims that he was spirited away on 14 May 1692. While more sceptical souls note simply that he died that day, tradition has him, still alive, and presumably still Minister of Aberfoyle, in fairyland.

1692

THE MASSACRE OF GLENCOE

Ever since the Revolution Settlement of 1689, there had been a belief in government circles that Jacobitism ought to be "rooted out" from among the clans who had supported James VII at Killiecrankie *(q.v.)*. For a while negotiation replaced intimidation and in August 1691 the western clan chiefs were offered indemnity if they took an oath of allegiance before 1 January 1692. It is unclear whether or not the offer was made in the hope of flushing out renegades, but at any rate the opportunity did arise to make an example of one small clan, the MacDonalds of Glencoe. The chief, MacIan, was a few days late in taking the oath and on the night of 13 February, 38 of the clan were treacherously murdered as they lay sleeping, by order of Dalrymple of Stair, King William's Scottish Secretary.

THE CONTEMPORARY VIEW

The winter time is the only season in which we are sure the Highlanders cannot escape and carry their wives, bairns and cattle to the hills. . . This is the proper time to maul them in the long dark nights.
                    Letter from Stair to the Earl of Breadalbane

THE WIDER VIEW

The massacre was carried out by Campbells but the guilt has to be shared among the highest in the land – it emerged that William was personally implicated. The "murder under trust" at Glencoe produced public indignation even in the Lowlands, notoriously unsympathetic to Highland squabbles and feudings, and Anglo-Scottish relations took another dip in the pre-Union period of tension. The MacDonalds were not martyrs in the Jacobite cause, though there would be many of them in years to come – but they do figure in the Scottish psyche, perhaps because of their association with an incredibly atmospheric sense of place.

THE FOUNDATION OF THE BANK OF SCOTLAND

Banking was traditionally associated with other forms of trade, for an example of this one may look to "Jingling Geordie" Heriot, the Edinburgh goldsmith and philanthropist who combined the role of jeweller and royal banker to James VI.

As trade and industry developed a more sophisticated form of banking service was thought necessary and Parliament in 1695 granted a new institution a monopoly of banking in Scotland for a 25 year period. The new Bank of Scotland's model was the Bank of England, founded by the Dumfriesshire-born William Paterson in 1694. Paterson was however hostile to the idea of a Scottish bank but became the moving force behind the Darien Scheme *(q.v.)*.

THE CONTEMPORARY VIEW

Our Soveraign Lord, considering how useful a Publick Bank may be in this Kingdom, according to the custom of other Kingdoms and States; and that the same can only be best set forth and managed by Persons in Company with a Joynt Stock, sufficiently indued with these Powers, and Authorities, and Liberties, necessary and usual in such Cases: Hath therefore Allowed, and, with the Advice and Consent of the Estates of Parliament, Allows a Joynt Stock, amounting to the Sum of Twelve Hundred Thousand Pounds Money, to be raised by the Company hereby Established. . .

Acts of the Parliament of Scotland, 1695

THE WIDER VIEW

The Bank of Scotland, or the "Old Bank" as it became known, enjoyed its monopoly for longer than planned, until 1727 when the New Bank, or Royal Bank of Scotland, was established to handle the financial affairs of the "Equivalent" – the payment made under the terms of the 1707 Treaty of Union *(q.v.)* which was intended, among other things, to compensate Scotland for assuming a share in the English National Debt.

1698

THE FIRST DARIEN EXPEDITION

On 14 July 1698 five ships of "The Company of Scotland Trading to Africa and the Indies" set sail from the port of Leith to the Isthmus of Darien in central America. On board were 1,200 would-be colonists. There were high hopes of regaining Scotland's traditional trading pre-eminence and challenging the English East India and Africa companies. Scotland would have her own colony and Darien, the "Door of the Seas, the Key of the Universe", was considered well placed to trade within the Americas and also to act as a staging post for the lucrative East Indies. The ambitious project, devised by William Paterson, was to be a panacea for Scotland's economic ills, excluded as she was from trade with England's colonies.

In just over a year the expedition was on its way back, a disaster, with more than half the Scots dead from fevers. Fort St Andrew in Caledonia Bay lay abandoned, still piled with useless trading goods. The English in Jamaica had refused to help and the sorry episode fuelled Scotland's sense of injustice.

THE CONTEMPORARY VIEW

Our men did not only continue dayly to grow more weakly and sickly but. . . we found severall species of the little provisions we had left . . . utterly spoylled and rotten. . . proclamations were publisht against us in Jamaica [which] prohibited. . . supplying or holding any sort of correspondence with us.

William Paterson's Report to the Directors of the Company

THE WIDER VIEW

The failure of two subsequent expeditions, hard upon the heels of the first, only served to deepen the wounds to the Scottish psyche. Many lost their lives, many more their savings as the scheme had enjoyed great national support. Anglo-Scottish relations were so bad that the idea of a more complete union seemed preposterous.

1705

THE *WORCESTER* AFFAIR

This violent episode, when an English vessel, the *Worcester*, was seized in the Firth of Forth in retaliation for a similar act against the last remaining ship belonging to the Company of Scotland, awakened resentful memories of the Darien Scheme *(q.v.)* The English captain, Green and two of his crew were, on the flimsiest of evidence, accused of piracy against the Company's *Speedy Return.* After a show trial in which the Edinburgh mob provided an intimidating chorus for the privy councillors and the vacillating government, the hapless Englishmen were hanged on the sands at Leith on 11 April 1705. Public opinion in Scotland was appeased but at the court of Queen Anne there was henceforth a new determination to do something about the unruly Scots, even if the Queen herself had done nothing more than urge the Scots Privy Council to delay execution, notably failing to issue a pardon.

THE CONTEMPORARY VIEW

Green was first execute. . . They every one of them, when the rope was about their necks, denied they were guilty of of that for which they were to die.

Wodrow: *Analecta* quoted in William Roughead
Riddle of the Ruthvens

If the Queen shall grant them remissions it will. . . so exasperate the nation as may render it difficult to make them join with England. . .

Letter from Baillie of Jerviswood to James Johnston
of Waristoun, quoted in Roughead.

THE WIDER VIEW

The *Worcester* affair followed hard upon the Scottish Parliament's Act of Security of 1704 in which the Scots refused to follow the English in nominating the Electress of Hanover and her heirs as the line of succession which would follow Queen Anne. The execution was the last violent deed in 700 years of bloody conflict before the Act of Union.

THE ACT OF UNION

From November 1706 until January 1707, while repeated petitions urged rejection of the union, the Scottish Parliament passed the articles of an Act which would bind together two ancient enemies, the final action of a parliament which had been an effective democratic legislature for less than twenty years.

The Scots' unenthusiasm for the French War and their refusal to agree to the dynastic succession embodied in the Act of Settlement (1701) threatened to destabilise the political situation. On occasions, such as the *Worcester* affair *(q.v.)*, war had looked likelier than union, and many, like Fletcher of Saltoun *(q.v.)*, even contemplated a republican solution. However 104 years of uneasy peace and broadly common Protestantism contributed to feelings, at least among those in power, that union was an idea whose moment had come. English suspicion that the Scots might play the French card led them to offer financial concessions and their guarantees anent the Kirk and the law were also significant. The negotiations coincided with a weak administration, many of whose leaders were indeed "bought and sold for English gold".

THE CONTEMPORARY VIEW

. . . I see a Free and Independent Kingdom delivering up That, which all the World has been fighting for. . . to wit, A Power to Manage their own Affairs by themselves. . .

Lord Belhaven: Debate on the Act of Union

THE WIDER VIEW

On 28 April the Scots Parliament was dissolved; "the end of an auld sang". Anglo-Scottish relations remained poor. Economic improvements were slow to arrive and neither country was happy. As Swift put it:

Strife and faction will o'erwhelm
Our crazy, double-bottomed realm.

However the Union would prove resilient enough to absorb the shocks of the Jacobite insurrections and most people settled for the Union they knew, if did not love.

THE "FIFTEEN"

The "old cause" of Jacobitism, in and out of fashion since the Revolution Settlement of 1688, was given a fresh urgency with the death of Queen Anne in 1714 and the succession of George I, the "wee German lairdie". France and Britain had been at peace since Utrecht in 1713 and all that James, the Old Pretender, could hope for was some Spanish support – that and hopes of a rebellion in sympathetic areas, beginning in Scotland and linking up with a rising in England. James's agent to bring this about was the Earl of Mar, "Bobbing John", a signatory to the Act of Union but now prepared to rebel against that Union.

The only significant engagements of the campaign were the surrender of the English Jacobites at Preston and the classic drawn battle of Sheriffmuir, near Dunblane, on 13 November.

THE CONTEMPORARY VIEW

Let my own tenants in Kildrummy know, that if they come not forth with their best arms, that I will send a party immediately to burn what they shall miss taking them.

Mar to his bailie

There's some say that we wan,
And some say that they wan
And some say that nane wan at a', man.

Anonymous song

For me it is no new thing to be unfortunate, since my whole life from my cradle has been a constant series of misfortunes.

James, the Old Pretender

THE WIDER VIEW

Mar's post-Sheriffmuir dallying at Perth, when he still possessed superior numbers, proved to be a fatal delay, since the clansmen melted away as quickly as they had responded to the fiery cross in September. It was an irrevocably disheartened force which met the Chevalier when he landed at Peterhead on 22 December, too late to affect the outcome.

THE DEATH OF ANDREW FLETCHER OF SALTOUN

Andrew Fletcher of Saltoun, who died in London in September 1716, had been one of the key figures in Scottish political life and thought in the years before the Union of 1707 *(q.v.)*.

Born in 1653, he represented East Lothian in the Scottish parliament intermittently from 1678. An opponent of the absolutist tendencies of James II and his ministers, he twice fled Scotland and joined the courts of Monmouth and William of Orange. His abiding political concern was the radical reform of Scotland which he saw as being only attainable through a substantial measure of political independence. A supporter of the Darien Scheme *(q.v.)*, he became a leader of the Parliamentary opposition to the Union, speaking bitterly of "the miserable condition to which this nation is reduced by its dependence on the English court".

After 1707 he withdrew, disappointed, from public life; devoting himself to agricultural improvements and his estate at Saltoun. His comment "if a man were permitted to make all the ballads, he need not care who should make the laws of a nation" has become famous.

THE CONTEMPORARY VIEW

. . . so steadfast to what he thought right that no hazard nor advantage . . . could tempt him to yield or desert it.

George Lockhart of Carnwath (Jacobite) on Fletcher

He would lose his life readily to serve his country; and would not do a base thing to save it.

John Macky (Whig) on Fletcher

THE WIDER VIEW

Fletcher's unchauvinistic patriotism, belief in a loose federal union and in the need for controls on royal authority, "If we may live free, I little value who is king", was ahead of its time, and his principled rejection of the 1707 Union marked him out from the venal majority of his fellow parliamentarians.

BATTLE OF GLENSHIEL

Survivors of the Jacobite Rising of 1715 *(q.v.)* joined the "Old Pretender" (James VIII & III *de jure*) and engaged in conspiracies around the Courts of Europe. The tense international situation favoured such intrigue. War had broken out between Britain and Spain in December 1718. In 1719 Spain planned an invasion of England, hoping to link up with English Jacobites. A diversionary raid with 300 Spanish troops and some exiled Scots Jacobites, led by the Earl Marischal, his brother James Keith and the Marquis of Tullibardine, was made on north west Scotland. Clan Mackenzie came out in support but few others moved.

On June 10/11 the 1500 strong Jacobite force was defeated by Government troops under General Wightman in Glenshiel. A nearby mountain now bears the name *Sgurr nan Spainteach* – the peak of the Spaniards.

THE CONTEMPORARY VIEW

. . . we came with hardly anything that was really necessary for such an undertaking. . .
        Marquis of Tullibardine to Earl of Mar 16th June 1719

. . . our troops were forced to retire to the top of the mountain. . .
the few troops they had had behaved in a manner not to give great
encouragement to try a second action. . . it was resolved the Spaniards
should surrender and the Highlanders disperse. . .
                        James Keith, Memoirs

THE WIDER VIEW

A diversionary attack on Wester Ross to support an English invasion may seem ill-judged, particularly as the Spanish Fleet met similar problems to the 1588 Armada and was dispersed by gales off Cape Finisterre. The 1719, apart from ruining the Mackenzies of Seaforth, emphasises that Jacobitism was more than a domestic dispute; it was part of European grand strategy and Spain and France waxed and waned in support of the "old cause" according to their perception of international affairs and national self-interest.

GENERAL WADE APPOINTED AS COMMANDER IN CHIEF, NORTH BRITAIN

In the aftermath of the Jacobite Risings of 1715 and 1719 *(q.v.)*, the 51-year-old Major General George Wade was appointed to investigate conditions in the Highlands, especially the effectiveness of the Disarming Act passed in 1716. Wade reported in December 1724 and recommended the establishment of companies of Highland troops under local officers, the building of a major fort at Inverness (Fort George) and another at the southern end of Loch Ness (Fort Augustus). He also noted the lack of good roads and bridges in the Highlands and the problems this caused in the movement of troops and the effective control of the area.

Wade was appointed Commander in Chief in the same month and during his 15½ years in this post he oversaw the building of some 250 miles of military roads and many bridges between Crieff and Dunkeld in the south and Inverness, Fort Augustus and Fort William.

THE CONTEMPORARY VIEW

If you had seen these roads before they were made
You'd hold up your hands and bless General Wade.

Contemporary rhyme

I presume to observe to your Majesty the great disadvantage which
regular troops are under when they engage with those who inhabit
mountainous situations. . . from want of Roads and Bridges, and
from the excessive rains that almost continuously fall in those parts. . .

Wade's Report

THE WIDER VIEW

Wade's roads, and the many more built by his less-famed successor Major William Caulfeild, have proved an enduring legacy and form the basis of many motor roads in the Highlands. It is ironic that the first use of them in time of war was during the 1745 Rising *(q.v.)* when the Jacobite Army gratefully used the road over the Corrieyairack on their southward march.

ALLAN RAMSAY PUBLISHES
THE GENTLE SHEPHERD

The Edinburgh wigmaker, bookseller, librarian and poet Allan Ramsay's most famous work is the pastoral comedy *The Gentle Shepherd*, a tale of country people set in the Pentland Hills. Ramsay (c.1685-1758) was a regular visitor to the Newhall area and very familiar with its people. His poem uniquely blends classical forms, realism and a warm sympathy for the life of his peasant protagonists.

Apart from its interest to literary historians, *The Gentle Shepherd* contains some of the most appealing Scottish poetry of the early eighteenth century. Its quality may be judged from the description of the waterfall at Habby's How:

> Go farer up the burn to Habby's How,
> Where a' the sweets of spring and summer grow;
> Between twa birks, out o'er a little lin
> The water fa's, and makes a singand din;
> A pool breast-deep beneath, as clear as glass,
> Kisses with easy whirles the bordring grass.

THE CONTEMPORARY VIEW

James Boswell (1740-95) was a Ramsay enthusiast and owned the original manuscript of *The Gentle Shepherd*. Perhaps predictably, his hero, Samuel Johnson, was less impressed. In the *Life of Johnson* Boswell wrote:

> I spoke of Allan Ramsay's "Gentle Shepherd". . . as the best
> pastoral that had ever been written. . . abounding with beautiful
> rural imagery. . . a real picture of manners; and I offered to teach
> Dr Johnson to understand it. "No, Sir (said he,) I won't learn it.
> You shall retain your superiority by my not knowing it."

THE WIDER VIEW

The Gentle Shepherd achieved enormous success with 20 editions appearing in Ramsay's lifetime and another 45 before 1800; and became, in ballad-opera form, a popular Scottish stage work. It marked a new approach to the depiction of the Scottish peasantry, a process continued 60 years later by Burns.

THE DEATH OF DANIEL DEFOE

Daniel Defoe, born in London in 1660, was one of the most versatile and prolific writers of his age. His involvement with Scotland formed a significant part of his life.

As one of the founders of the English novel he is now best remembered as the author of *Robinson Crusoe* – an adventure story, with a strong infusion of ethics and philosophy, inspired by the remarkable experiences of a Scottish sailor, Alexander Selkirk, from Largo, Fife. Selkirk was a buccaneer who was voluntarily marooned on Juan Fernández island off the coast of South America. Selkirk's history became famous, the essayist Richard Steele giving an account of his adventures in 1713. Defoe's novel appeared in 1719.

Years before, Defoe had been sent to Scotland, around the period of the Union of Parliaments, to act as a spy and undercover political agent for the English government.

THE CONTEMPORARY VIEW

I was exceedingly surprized with the print of a man's naked foot on the shore, which was very plain to be seen in the sand.

Defoe, *Robinson Crusoe*

The four principal streets are the fairest for breadth and the finest built that I have ever seen in one city together. . . In a word, 'tis the cleanest and beautifullest and best built city in Britain, London excepted.

Defoe's description of Glasgow from, *A Tour through the Whole Island of Great Britain*

THE WIDER VIEW

Defoe's *Tour*, published between 1724 and 1726, is a valuable description of post-Union Scotland. That Defoe lived to write *Robinson Crusoe* and the *Tour* is testimony to his expertise in espionage. His intelligence work had not been suspected in Scotland or else in the words of Sir John Clerk of Penicuik "the mob of Edinburgh had pulled him to pieces".

THE ORIGINAL SECESSION

The 1689/90 Revolution Settlement secured the presbyterian Church of Scotland as the established church. Links between Church and State were close, as were connections with local landowners. Landowners or heritors had a duty to maintain ecclesiastical buildings and enjoyed considerable influence in church affairs, particularly over patronage, or the appointment of ministers. This led to conflict with those who valued the right of ordinary parishioners to choose their pastor.

In 1731 the Church's General Assembly declared that only heritors and elders might vote in the election of ministers. In December 1733 a Stirling minister, Ebenezer Erskine, who had campaigned against this decision, was suspended by the Assembly and left to form the Secession Church, which won considerable support in the Lowlands.

The Secessionists' factional tendencies weakened them. A split in 1744 on the Burgess Oath, which obliged potential burgesses in some Royal Burghs to pledge support for the established religion, created Burgher and Anti-Burgher parties. Later each of these groups split into Old Light and New Light blocs, over State support for the Church.

THE CONTEMPORARY VIEW

The promoters of that schism appear to have been harsh, narrow-minded men. . . they had an unhappy talent at splitting hairs, and of taking offence at persons and things without a cause.

John Ramsay of Auchtertyre (1736-1814), *Diaries*

(Ramsay was a prosperous landowner and writes of the Secession from the perspective of the Established Church.)

THE WIDER VIEW

The patronage issue continued to disturb the Kirk for another 141 years, leading to the Disruption of 1843 *(q.v.)* The Relief Church, more liberal in outlook than the Secessionists, founded by Thomas Gillespie in 1761, was another product of the patronage controversy, a conflict only ended by an Act of Parliament passed in 1874.

THE PORTEOUS RIOTS

Disorder was never far from the streets of Edinburgh and the Porteous Riots of 1736 shows the potential for mob rule. The policing of Edinburgh was entrusted to a paramilitary City Guard, nicknamed the "black banditti". This force was largely Highland in origin and violent in disposition.

In April 1736 John Porteous, Captain of the City Guard, was on duty at the execution in the Grassmarket of Andrew Wilson, a smuggler. After the execution a minor affray broke out and on Porteous's orders the Guard opened fire; deaths and injuries ensued. Porteous stood trial for murder, was found guilty but granted a Royal Pardon. On 19 July an outraged mob broke into the Tolbooth, seized Porteous and hung him from a dyer's pole in the Grassmarket.

The incident was used by Walter Scott in *The Heart of Midlothian*.

THE CONTEMPORARY VIEW

[Porteous] *by his skill in manly exercises, particularly the golf, and by gentlemanly behaviour, was admitted into the company of his superiors, which elated his mind, and added insolence to his native roughness, so that he was much hated and feared by the mob of Edinburgh.*

Alexander Carlyle, *Autobiography*

THE WIDER VIEW

The crowd's evident partiality for Wilson reflects both sympathy for the smuggler and perhaps post-Union distaste for central Government. London reacted strongly, assuming civic complicity, and the House of Lords instituted an enquiry into the lynching and the administration of justice in Scotland. The Lord Provost was summoned south to answer for the affair, disqualified from office and the City fined. The Porteous affair marks a growing tension between between Prime Minister Walpole and the Duke of Argyll who had been a key Government supporter but whose defence of the Edinburgh authorities distanced him from Walpole.

THE RAISING OF THE
BLACK WATCH

Companies of irregular Highland troops had long been used by the Government to help control their unruly neighbours but, as the events of the Jacobite Rising of 1715 *(q.v.)* had proved them to be of little practical value, they were disbanded in 1717. As part of General Wade's report on Highland affairs in 1724 *(q.v.)* he recommended the raising of new Highland Companies, under local officers and subject to martial law. Wade's proposals were accepted and six Companies were raised in 1725. Uniformed in dark "government" tartan they became colloquially known as *Am Freiceadan Dubh*, the Black Watch, to distinguish them from the regular *Saighdearan Dearg*, the red soldiers. These units were, in 1739, formed into a regular infantry regiment, the Highland Regiment of Foot (later, and better, if variously, known as the 42nd Foot, the Royal Highland Regiment, The Black Watch).

THE CONTEMPORARY VIEW

They are a hardy and intrepid race, and no great mischief if they fall.
General James Wolfe on Highland soldiers

I am for having always in our army as many Scottish soldiers as possible; not that I think them more brave. . . but because they are generally more hardy and less mutinous: and of all Scottish soldiers I should choose to have and keep. . . as many Highlanders as possible.
Lord Barrington (Secretary at War), 1751

THE WIDER VIEW

The Highlands and Islands became a great pool of manpower from which the expanding British Empire drew soldiers. Wallace Notestein in *The Scot in History* says that from 1797 to 1837 the Island of Skye alone gave to the British Army 21 generals, 48 lieutenant colonels and 600 other commissioned officers and 10,000 other ranks. The resident population of Skye in 1821 was just under 21,000.

1740

THE COMPLETION OF THE PUBLICATION OF HUME'S *TREATISE ON HUMAN NATURE*

In a golden age of Scottish intellectual life the figure of David Hume (1711–76) stands supreme. Philosopher, historian, librarian and diplomat, his first major work, the *Treatise on Human Nature*, is often described as the greatest work by a British philosopher. Its ambitious aim was to define a complete philosophical system, an objective in keeping with Enlightenment ideas.

The work, published in three parts in 1739 and 1740, in Hume's own words "fell stillborn from the press". However, later works achieved more public success, although Hume's religious scepticism blocked his appointment to professorships at Edinburgh and Glasgow. His anti-establishment image did not prevent his appointment as Librarian of the Advocates' Library in Edinburgh between 1751 and 1757, employment on diplomatic missions to France or filling a senior post in the Home Department in 1767/68.

THE CONTEMPORARY VIEW

I have always considered him, both in his life-time and since his death, as approaching as nearly to the idea of a perfectly wise and virtuous man as perhaps the nature of human frailty will permit.

Adam Smith of David Hume

How much better are you than your books!

Said by James Boswell to David Hume

. . . a man who has so little scrupulosity as to venture to oppose those principles which have been thought necessary to human happiness.

Samuel Johnson of David Hume

THE WIDER VIEW

Hume was part of a remarkable flowering of Scottish philosophical thought extending from the 1730s through Adam Smith *(q.v.)* in the later eighteenth century to Dugald Stewart in the 1820s. The empiricism which underlies Hume's thinking, seeking as it did rational explanations for sociological and economic phenomena, became a particularly Scottish philosophical characteristic.

THE FOUNDATION OF THE LEADHILLS LIBRARY

The Lanarkshire mining village of Leadhills in the Lowther Hills saw a novel experiment in 1741 – the provision of a circulating library run by and for the lead-miners. Probably founded by James Stirling, a distinguished mathematician, who was manager of the mines, the library continued as an autonomous working-class institution into the modern era.

The stock was dominated by works on history and religion and its impact on the community and the extent to which the formidably intellectual contents were used by the miners was a matter of widespread comment. Dorothy Wordsworth, on her Scottish tour with William in 1803, heard reports of Leadhills as a "large library of long standing". The library later bore the name of Alan Ramsay, the author of *The Gentle Shepherd (q.v.)*, a native of Leadhills.

THE CONTEMPORARY VIEW

Having. . . a great deal of spare time, they employ themselves in reading, and for this purpose have been at the expence of fitting up a library, out of which everyone who contributes to the expence receives boooks.

Statistical Account of Crawford Parish, 1791

THE WIDER VIEW

Leadhills was followed by its near-neighbour, Wanlockhead, where miners established a "Society for Purchasing Books in Wanlockhead" in 1756. These were not the first lending libraries, the 1704 General Assembly having supported a plan outlined by Rev. James Kirkwood in his *Overture for founding and maintaining of bibliothecks in every paroch throughout this Kingdom,* published in 1699. This was an ambitious and far-sighted plan of limited impact, in part due to the tiny size of the parochial libraries established. Other charitable foundations existed in towns from Kirkwall to Edinburgh. The special characteristic of the Leadhills and Wanlockhead Libraries was their foundation for, financial support and extensive use by, an almost exclusively working-class clientele.

THE KILLING OF THE LAST WOLF IN SCOTLAND

There never were any wolves on the Island of Harris, if Monro's *Description of the Western Isles* (c.1548) is to believed. The implication of this is that the wolf (*Canis lupus*) was still widespread elsewhere in the Hebrides.

Of course there is no real need to speculate about these matters, other than to gain a clue about the comparative wildness of Scotland right up to the eighteenth century. Certainly, the several tales about the fate of the "last wolf" lie very much in the realm of folklore or early "tourist trappery". Nevertheless. . .

The last wolf in Scotland was said by Pennant (1775) to have been killed near Killiecrankie in 1680 by Sir Ewan Cameron of Lochiel. However another account has it that the last of the species had the *coup de grace* from one Eagan Macqueen on the lands of the Mackintosh of Mackintosh, Inverness-shire in 1743. By a strange coincidence the clan crest of Macqueen is the only one to show a wolf.

THE CONTEMPORARY VIEW

Macqueen of Corrybrough. Crest badge: A wolf rampant ermine holding a pheon gules point downwards argent.

> *I buckled with him and dirked him and syne whittled his craig and brought away his countenance for fear that he might come alive again.*
>
> Macqueen the gillie

THE WIDER VIEW

The sobriquet given in the reign of Robert III to his brother, Alexander, Earl of Buchan, the "Wolf of Badenoch", shows the extent to which the animal was seen as synonymous with the kind of terrors of one who burned Elgin Cathedral because of a dispute with the Bishop of Moray. An atavistic fear of the wolf may frustrate plans to reintroduce the species into the Highlands as a useful predator on the over-numerous red deer population.

THE LANDING OF THE
YOUNG PRETENDER

On 23 July 1745 Prince Charles Edward Stewart landed on the island of Eriskay in the Outer Hebrides; two days later he and his pitifully small band of companions – the Seven Men of Moidart – reached the mainland. Jacobitism, which had provided an insistent refrain throughout a century of British politics, was about to reach its final crescendo, beginning and ending in Scotland. A strange symmetry of events saw Charles take his final leave on ship to France from Loch nam Uamh, close by to Moidart, just over a year later.

The tale has often been told of how some of the clans were won over to the Prince's side, how the standard was raised at Glenfinnan on 19 August and how less than a month later he was in Edinburgh without meeting serious resistance. The absence of French assistance remained a handicap to the cause and there was no substantial support from citizens of Edinburgh, however much a few ladies' hearts might flutter at the romantic figure of the Prince. This was still true, even after the resounding Jacobite victory at Prestonpans, outside Edinburgh, when General Cope was put to ignominious flight.

"With these, as matters stand. . . I must either conquer or perish in a little while". So said Charles when deciding to cross the Border. No more reinforcements could be expected from Scotland but he hoped the Army would be swelled by the many English and Welsh who professed to be adherents of James VIII. Charles was to be sadly disappointed in this, but first-rate advice from Lord George Murray and a clever feint to march down the east coast enabled the Prince to reach Derby, only 130 miles from London. Panic gripped the capital, which lay open to a further thrust, but at Derby Charles's advisers forced on him the decision to turn back – a decision which has led to the immense poignancy of the unfulfilled possibilities of the '45. On 19 December they re-crossed the Border – Culloden lay four months off.

THE CONTEMPORARY VIEW

Lochiel, whom my father esteemed the best friend of our family, may stay at home, and learn his Prince's fate from the newspapers.

> Charles to Cameron of Lochiel, when the
> latter asked him to call off the enterprise

*I'll share the fate of my Prince and so shall every man over whom nature
or fortune has given me any power.*

Lochiel's reply

*Hey, Johnnie Cope, are ye wauking yet
Or are your drums a-beating yet?
If ye were wauking I wad wait
To gang to the coals i' the morning.*

Adam Skirving: "Johnnie Cope"

*[Charles] fell into a passion and gave most of the gentlemen that spoke
very abusive language and said that they had a mind to betray him.*

Lord Elcho's account of the Prince's response
on being counselled to retreat from Derby

I can see nothing but ruin and destruction to us in case we should retreat.

Prince Charles Edward Stewart

THE WIDER VIEW

The religious and cultural divisions in Scottish society were revealed
by the hostility of most Lowland Scots to the prince. Even in the
Highlands there was reluctance to take part in an ill-equipped
adventure which many felt could only bring disappointment and
worse to those who took the great gamble and "came out" for the
Stewarts. These divisions were deepened by the '45 and the whole
political and social fabric of the Highlands wrecked, leaving little of
Jacobitism save, in Maurice Lindsay's phrase "a passionate nostalgia".

THE FAILURE OF THE JACOBITE REBELLION

The Jacobite army which turned back from Derby and recrossed the Border in December 1745 was still an effective force – the rearguard action conducted by Lord George Murray was followed by a brilliant action against Hawley at Falkirk. After this the rebel force began to deteriorate while the King's son, the Duke of Cumberland, moved northwards with another army. Unable to capture Stirling, Charles retreated beyond the Highland line and on 16 April 1746 he chose to give battle on Drummossie Moor, Culloden. The half-starved and exhausted clansmen, on ground unsuited to the Highland charge, were routed, a thousand died on the field and many more in the days and weeks which followed, as Cumberland earned his nickname of "Butcher". No quarter was the order of the day and the atrocities were not committed by the English alone, since a sizeable part of Cumberland's forces were Scotsmen.

THE CONTEMPORARY VIEW

Never was more improper ground for Highlanders than that where we fought

> Lord George Murray to Charles in a letter
> on the day after the battle

*Would to God the enemy had been worthy enough of our troops. . .
Silence and obedience the whole time and our manoeuvres were
performed without the least confusion. I must own that you have hit
my weak side when you say that the honour of our troops is restored;
that pleases me beyond all honours due to me.*

> Cumberland to Sir John Ligonier

THE WIDER VIEW

The aftermath of defeat in battle was the dismantling of a way of life. The disintegration of the old Highland society was achieved by a series of Acts which removed the patriarchal authority of the chiefs, and removed their military threat by proscription of arms and even of Highland dress.

THE ABOLITION OF
HERITABLE JURISDICTION

Following Culloden, the Government declared the lands of many of the Jacobite chiefs forfeit. This was only part of the most sustained and systematic programme of pacification which had followed any of the series of rebellions. Under the Disarming Act of 1746 all weapons of any sort were to be given up and new impositions striking at the very heart of Highland culture were introduced; the wearing of Highland Dress was banned and playing of the Great Pipes proscribed. The pipes were treated in this way because they were said to be "an instrument of war".

In a general reform of Scots law and government the office of Secretary of State was abolished and the "heritable jurisdictions" of landowners, which had been guaranteed under the Act of Union *(q.v.)*, were revoked. This removed from the clan chiefs the feudal powers of "gallows and pit" which extended to every offence except treason. Hereditary sheriffs had similar enforced reductions in judicial authority and power gradually passed to the lawyers and the government officials.

THE CONTEMPORARY VIEW

There was perhaps never any change of national manners so quick, so great, and so general as that which operated in the Highlands by the last conquest and the subsequent laws.

Samuel Johnson, *A Journey to the Western Islands of Scotland* (1775)

THE WIDER VIEW

Culloden and its aftermath is a story of a determined policy of enforced cultural change backed by the power of the state. The old values of the clan system were removed as effectively as Dr Johnson suggested, but there were further consequences, including large-scale emigration which he also observed. "To govern peaceably by having no subjects is an expedient that argues no great profundity of policy."

1748

THE PUBLICATION OF TOBIAS SMOLLETT'S *RODERICK RANDOM*

Smollett's first novel was, to a large extent, a version of his own early years and career. Born at Place of Bonhill, near Dumbarton, in 1721, he became a surgeon and went to London in the hope of becoming a playwright, then, forestalled in this, took ship with the navy against the Spaniards in the West Indies. He was present at the attack on Cartagena and saw violent action which he graphically describes in *Roderick Random* and other later writings. This and other of his novels were much admired in the eighteenth century; in recent years American scholarship has rehabilitated Smollett's reputation, which had waned in the intervening years.

THE CONTEMPORARY VIEW

The reader gratifies his curiosity in pursuing the adventures of a person in whose favour he is prepossessed; he espouses his cause, he sympathises with him in distress. . . and every impression having a double force on the imagination, the memory retains the circumstance, and the heart improves by the example.

Smollett, Preface to *Roderick Random*

. . . we had rich enough conversation on literary subjects, which was enlivened by Smollett's agreeable stories, which he told with peculiar grace.

Alexander Carlyle, *Autobiography*

THE WIDER VIEW

Smollett's place in the history of the novel is today seen as being comparable with that of Henry Fielding. He favoured a fairly loose episodic and picaresque structure but added to this tremendous vitality, humour and a flair for story-telling. The first of Scottish novelists, his impact at home was negligible, by reason of self-imposed exile, although he illuminated the pages of his masterpiece *Humphry Clinker* (his last novel) with an account of his last visit to his native land. Much earlier he had lamented oppression in his Culloden-inspired poem "The Tears of Scotland".

THE APPIN MURDER

In the aftermath of the 1745 Rising *(q.v.)* the forfeited estates of Jacobite leaders were administered by government factors. One such factor was Colin Campbell of Glenure, who in May 1752 was shot by a hidden marksman while collecting rents on the Appin estates of Clan Cameron and Stewart of Ardsheil.

After much inquiry, one James Stewart, "James of the Glens" was arrested and charged with being an accessory to the murder – the actual killer never being arrested, although a soldier in the French service, Alan Breck Stewart, was named as the murderer. Alan Breck had been an intermediary between his exiled clan chief and his tenants who were paying double rents – one to the Government and one to Stewart. James of the Glens was tried at Inveraray, executed and his body for years afterwards hung from a gibbet at Ballachulish. Alan Breck escaped to France. Highland tradition has a long list of alternative assassins.

THE CONTEMPORARY VIEW

This is a Campbell that's been killed. Well, it'll be tried in Inverara, the Campbell's head place; with fifteen Campbell's in the jury-box, and the biggest Campbell of all (and that's the Duke) sitting cocking on the bench. . . what would the clan think if there was a Campbell shot and naebody hanged, and their own chief the Justice General.

Robert Louis Stevenson, *Kidnapped*

THE WIDER VIEW

The Appin Murder controversy has endured for close on two and half centuries. It has also inspired two of Scotland's best-loved novels: *Kidnapped* and *Catriona*. Stevenson's interest in the murder owes much to legends he heard on childhood visits to the Highlands. His description, given above, of the probable trial the killer of Colin Campbell could expect, is a not unfair description of the actual hearing.

THE FOUNDATION OF THE CARRON IRONWORKS

The village of Carron, near Falkirk, saw the origins of large-scale iron-making in Scotland. Iron had previously been produced in small, often rural, sites, governed by the availability of wood to be turned into charcoal – the eponymous village of Furnace on Loch Fyneside is an example. In 1759 William Cadell Snr, his son William Jnr, Samuel Garbett and Dr John Roebuck established an ironwork, utilising local ores and coal and the coke-smelting process developed by Abraham Darby at Coalbrookdale earlier in the century. The Carron Company grew to become one of the largest concerns in Scotland and was closely associated with James Watt's early experiments *(q.v.)*.

THE CONTEMPORARY VIEW

Permission is got at the inn, for liberty to visit these terrifying works. The heat and illumination from the burning materials, the roaring blasts, and the noise of the weighty hammers, make impressions upon a stranger, not easily described. This was the first company of the kind in Scotland; it is chartered, and has a capital of £150,000.

The Traveller's Guide through Scotland and it's
(sic) Islands, 4th ed., Edinburgh 1808

We cam' na here to view your warks, In hope to be mair wise, But only, lest we gang to hell; It may be nae surprise

Robert Burns, *Verses written on a window of the Inn at Carron.* (1787)

THE WIDER VIEW

The Carron Company was central to the Industrial Revolution in Scotland, for example building the engine for the pioneering steamship *Charlotte Dundas*. The company was a sponsor of the Forth and Clyde Canal *(q.v.)* whose eastern terminus was on the Carron River. The company's most famous product was the "Carronade" – a short-range large-calibre cannon widely used by the Royal Navy during the French Revolutionary and Napoleonic Wars.

1761

THE PUBLICATION OF
MACPHERSON'S *FINGAL*

The publication by a young Inverness-shire schoolmaster, James Macpherson (1736-96), of *Fingal: an ancient epic poem* created an unprecedented literary sensation and controversy. In 1760 Macpherson had published to great acclaim *Fragments of Ancient Poetry Collected in the Highlands of Scotland* – a collection of Gaelic oral tradition poetry. On the strength of this work he was commissioned to tour the Highlands in search of the supposed epic poem of the adventures of the Celtic hero, Fingal, as told by his son Ossian. *Fingal* and *Temora* (1763) were the fruits of these travels. However suspicion swiftly grew that they owed more to Macpherson than to genuine oral tradition. Modern opinion suggests that a small core of genuine ancient verse was arranged, supplemented and built on by Macpherson to produce an epic in a style designed to appeal to eighteenth century sensibilities.

THE CONTEMPORARY VIEW

Ossian, sublimest, simplest bard of all
Whom English infidels, Macpherson call
Charles Churchill, *The Prophecy of Famine* (1763)

I believe they [the Ossian poems] *never existed in any other form than that which we have seen. The editor, or author, never could shew the original. . .*
Samuel Johnson, *A Journey to the Western Islands* (1775)

THE WIDER VIEW

The absence of a written original, Dr Johnson's point, is of course unsurprising in an oral tradition – a type of culture Johnson was unused to. Forgery or not, the Ossianic poems took Europe by storm. They were swiftly translated into all the main European languages, even Polish and Hungarian. A French translation accompanied Napoleon Bonaparte on his campaigns. The Highlands of Scotland became a place of fantasy and imagination, intrepid travellers began to penetrate the lonely glens and sea-lochs where they believed the Fingalian warriors had fought and loved.

THE NEW TOWN OF EDINBURGH

In May 1767 an Act of Parliament extended Edinburgh's boundaries northwards over the Nor' Loch (now drained to form Princes Street Gardens) and then in the process of being bridged. James Craig (1740-95) won the competition for the design plans for the New Town.

The Old Town, built around the ridge running from the Castle to Holyrood, was densely built, insanitary and chaotic. The New Town expressed Enlightenment ideas of planning, symmetry and elegance and reflected classical influences and in particular the works of the sixteenth-century Italian architect Andrea Palladio. It would be a suburb for the wealthy, introducing spatial separation of socio-economic groups, a sharp contrast to the close proximity in which the different classes had lived in the Old Town.

THE CONTEMPORARY VIEW

. . . on the 3rd of June the magistrates complimented Mr James Craig, architect, with a gold medal, and with the freedom of the city in a silver box, as an acknowledgement of his merit in his having designed the best plan of the new town; the ground was afterwards marked out into proper plots for building,. . . as the bridge of communication, which is now well advanced, is to be finished in about two years, it is probable the building will soon begin, so as the houses may be habitable by the time the bridge is finished.

Scots Magazine, August 1767

THE WIDER VIEW

Edinburgh's New Town was not the first planned development in a Scottish city. Glasgow's earlier westward development from its medieval core into the Merchant City displays similar regularity of design and Palladian architecture. Edinburgh's New Town however enjoyed the services of the greatest architect of the Georgian period, Robert Adam (1728-92), whose Charlotte Square and Register House are master-pieces of European architecture.

PUBLICATION OF THE POEMS OF DUNCAN BÀN MACINTYRE

A poet unable to write down his own poetry, a gamekeeper conscripted as an unwilling soldier in the Hanoverian army, a member of the Edinburgh City Guard, turned soldier again. An unlikely enough background, but one which produced some of the finest Gaelic poetry of the eighteenth century, a century and a genre not lacking in excellence – for example Alasdair MacDonald (Alasdair MacMhaighstir Alasdair)'s "Birlinn of Clanranald". Among Macintyre's poems the best known is perhaps "Moladh Beinn Dobhrain" (In praise of Ben Dorain) – a long evocation of nature which has a formal structure based on the classical music of the Highland bagpipes, the pibroch or *ceol mor*.

Macintyre was born in 1724 in Glen Orchy and died in Edinburgh in 1812.

THE CONTEMPORARY VIEW

When she lifteth her voice,
What joy 'tis to hear
The ghost of her breath
As it echoeth clear.
For she calleth aloud,
From the cliff of the crag,
Her silver-hipped lover,
The proud-antlered stag.
Well-antlered, high-headed,
Loud voiced doth he come,
From the haunts he well knows
Of Bendorain his home.

    "The Haunt of the Deer" – John Campbell
    Shairp's translation of "Praise of Ben Dorain"

THE WIDER VIEW

The original publication of the poems, their success and the production of further editions in his lifetime is indicative of a changing and warmer attitude to Gaeldom and the Highlands in the decades after the '45 Rising *(q.v.)* and the ending of the perceived Jacobite threat. Indeed one of Macintyre's poems celebrates the repeal of the 35-year-old ban on Highland dress in 1782.

JAMES WATT PATENTS THE SEPARATE CONDENSER FOR STEAM ENGINES

James Watt, born in Greenock in 1736, like many contemporary engineers turned his hand to several areas of activity. His major achievement is the separate condenser which dramatically improved the efficiency of steam engines.

Trained in Glasgow, he became mathematical instrument maker to Glasgow University in 1757. While repairing a Newcomen steam engine around 1763 he devised the separate condenser and various other improvements. He left the University and worked with John Roebuck of the Carron Iron Works *(q.v.)* on a colliery engine. He then formed a partnership with Matthew Boulton and in 1775 began manufacturing steam engines at Boulton's works at Soho, near Birmingham. Through Watt's patent the partners established a virtual monopoly of steam engine manufacture.

Watt became rich and famous. His prestige was enormous and his word on engineering matters was law; however Watt had one blind spot, an aversion to the idea of steam power applied to transport. He warned Henry Bell, of *Comet (q.v.)* fame against applying steam power to ships and William Murdock was discouraged from experimenting with steam locomotion. Watt retired in 1800 when his Patent expired. He died in 1819.

THE CONTEMPORARY VIEW

. . . JAMES WATT, Who directing the Force of an Original Genius Early exercised in Philosophic Research To the Improvement of the Steam Engine, Enlarged the Resources of his Country, Increased the Power of Man, and Rose to an Eminent Place, Among the most illustrious Followers of Science, and the Real Benefactors of the World.
Inscription on Watt's Monument in Westminster Abbey

THE WIDER VIEW

Watt did not "invent the steam engine"; he did greatly improve it and made what had been, in its earlier, less efficient form, mainly a pumping engine, into the Industrial Revolution's motive force and symbol.

"GLASGOW MADE THE CLYDE, AND THE CLYDE MADE GLASGOW"

Until the early nineteenth century ocean-going ships could not come up the Clyde to Glasgow and their cargoes were transhipped at ports downstream. The deepening of the river and the encouragement of trade were priorities of the City Council and eminent engineers such as John Smeaton and James Watt were commissioned to prepare schemes to improve the navigation of the river. In 1770 an Act of Parliament created the Clyde Trust to give effect to the plans of John Golbourne, a Chester engineer. Golbourne's elegant solution combined dredging with the use of the river to deepen itself. He built jetties or groynes which speeded the flow of water and thus scoured silt and mud from the river.

By 1775 vessels drawing 6 feet could reach the city's Broomielaw Harbour and in 1806 a 150 ton schooner discharged cargo from Lisbon there. However, in 1812, Henry Bell's little *Comet (q.v.)* managed to run aground on her maiden voyage. The struggle to deepen and manage the Clyde was an endless one but without the Clyde Trust's work Glasgow could not have developed as a major industrial centre.

THE CONTEMPORARY VIEW

I found Glasgow greatly enlarged; I was there eleven years previous to this tour, and I could hardly believe it possible for a town to be so increased in size and improved as it was in 1796.
    Sarah Murray, *The Beauties of Scotland* (1799)

THE WIDER VIEW

The full benefits of the Clyde Trust's work came with the development of shipyards and docks in the very heart of the city. Launches of great ships like the record-breaking 3,700 ton *Persia* from Robert Napier's Govan shipyard in 1855 were only made possible by the process initiated in 1770.

THE PUBLICATION OF
ENCYCLOPÆDIA BRITANNICA

The first edition of the oldest and largest English language encyclopædia was issued in Edinburgh by the "Society of Gentlemen in Scotland" in instalments or numbers between 1768 and 1771. The printer and first editor was William Smellie and the major themes of the first edition were the arts and sciences. Later editions added history and biography. Various publishing houses took over responsibility for the encyclopædia and from 1929 it has had a transatlantic ownership. From that date it has been continuously revised rather than appearing in different editions. It remains a major work of scholarship and reference.

THE CONTEMPORARY VIEW

Enclyclopedia Britannica; or, a DICTIONARY of ARTS and SCIENCES, compiled upon a new plan. In which the different SCIENCES and ARTS are digested into distinct Treatises or Systems; and the various TECHNICAL TERMS, &c. are explained as they occur in the order of the Alphabet. Illustrated with One Hundred and Sixty Copperplates.

Title Page of Volume 1 of the first edition
of the Encyclopædia Britannica (1768)

THE WIDER VIEW

The word "encyclopædia" means "instruction in the whole circle of learning". Diderot and D'Alembert in France had issued *L'Encyclopedie* between 1751 and 1776. This publication was seen as a symbol of rational thought and attracted contributors of the highest intellectual ability, such as Rousseau and Montesquieu. It was unsurprising that Scotland imitated France and produced the first English-language encyclopædia. Edinburgh was at the height of its fame as the centre of the Scottish Enlightenment, the "Athens of the North", and Scottish scholars and philosophers of the day consciously looked to France for their intellectual and cultural models. Scotland continued to have a great tradition in the production of encyclopædias. In 1859, Robert Chambers, of W. & R. Chambers in Edinburgh issued Chambers' Encyclopædia.

BOSWELL AND JOHNSON'S TOUR OF THE HEBRIDES

In the summer of 1773 James Boswell, advocate, diarist and later author of the most famous biography in the English language, persuaded the subject of that biography, Dr Samuel Johnson, the great English man of letters and "celebrity", to spend four months with him in Scotland. In August they embarked on an extensive and astonishing (given Johnson's age of 64, corpulence and sedentary habits) tour which took them up the East coast and across to the Western Highlands and Islands.

THE CONTEMPORARY VIEW

It was a delightful day. Loch Ness, and the road upon the side of it, between birch trees, with the hills above, pleased us much. The scene was as remote and agreeably wild as could be desired. . . To see Mr Johnson in any new situation is an object of attention to me. As I saw him now for the first time ride along. . . I thought of "London, a Poem", of "The Rambler", of "False Alarm"; and I cannot express the ideas which went across my imagination.

James Boswell: Manuscript of his *Journal of a Tour to the Hebrides*

. . . whatever makes the past, the distant, or the future predominate over the present, advances us in the dignity of thinking beings. . . That man is little to be envied, whose patriotism would not gain force upon the plain of Marathon, or whose piety would not grow warmer among the ruins of Iona!

Samuel Johnson, *A Journey to the Western Islands of Scotland*

THE WIDER VIEW

Both men later published successful accounts of their impressions, Boswell as ever noting little intimate details of the reaction of his father-figure to the alien scenes and customs among which they journeyed, while Johnson gives an acute and sometimes moving account of a society in disintegration.

THE BUILDING OF REGISTER HOUSE BY ROBERT ADAM

Robert, the second son of William, born in Kirkcaldy in 1728, brought the Adam name to its chief glory with his achievements as an architect. With the design for Register House, which faces the Old Town from across the North Bridge, he brought to Edinburgh the talents which had already won him a European reputation. Built to house the public records of Scotland, Adam's creation shows its classical origins and his earlier manner in its simple but elegant lines and use of the rising ground.

Like other *illuminati* of the Enlightenment, Adam sought his inspiration from Italy. He went on the Grand Tour, lived and worked in Rome and attained such fame that he received an invitation to plan the rebuilding of Lisbon after the earthquake of 1755. Much of his reputation was gained and his work carried out in England, but his influence on both the old and new towns of Edinburgh was significant.

THE CONTEMPORARY VIEW

Robert had been three years in Italy, and, with a first-rate genius for his profession, had seen and studied everything, and was in the highest esteem among foreign artists. From the time of his return. . . may be dated a very remarkable improvement in building and furniture. . .
Alexander Carlyle, *Autobiography*

THE WIDER VIEW

Almost two decades later Adam was still helping to shape his own capital city. In the old town he created the Old Quadrangle of the University (1789) - to be completed by Playfair – and, as a culmination of a furious burst of energy, his Charlotte Square (1791) completed the year before his death, provides the centre piece for James Craig's New Town *(q.v.)*. It is a broad and stately space even today, enhanced by a conservation scheme, if not by traffic management.

THE PUBLICATION OF ADAM SMITH'S *WEALTH OF NATIONS*

Adam Smith, regarded as a founder of the science of political economy, saw himself as a philosopher in a time when philosophy embraced disciplines as diverse as mathematics, theology and politics. Although today often seen as an arch-apostle of capitalism, Smith's view of economic self-interest is linked with the social needs of the community.

Born in Kirkcaldy in 1723, Smith made his reputation when he published *The Theory of Moral Sentiments.* This brought him the patronage of the Duke of Buccleuch. On becoming tutor to the Duke who he accompanied on the Grand Tour, Smith resigned the Chair of Moral Philosophy at Glasgow, which he had held since 1752. As Professor he had delivered the lectures which formed the basis of *An Inquiry into the Nature and Causes of the Wealth of Nations.* In it he champions the division of labour – so that commerce be advanced by specific things being done exceptionally well. Freedom of commerce and industry are advocated with an enlightened society as the objective.

THE CONTEMPORARY VIEW

To found a great empire for the sole purpose of raising up a people of customers, may at first sight appear a project fit only for a nation of shopkeepers. It is, however, a project altogether unfit for a nation of shopkeepers; but extremely fit for a nation that is governed by shopkeepers.

The Wealth of Nations

THE WIDER VIEW

Today we find Smith difficult to classify and his masterpiece has become an anachronistic handbook for Wall Street and right-wing politicians. Smith has been cast in a political role he would not have sought. He is better viewed as one of the chief adornments of the eighteenth century Scottish Enlightenment, resembling his contemporary David Hume in his powerful rational thought.

THE DEATH OF ALLAN RAMSAY

Son of Allan Ramsay the poet *(q.v.)*, the younger Ramsay became Scotland's first internationally known artist and advanced the art of portraiture both north and south of the Border. Trained in the tradition of master and apprentice, he also saw art as part of a general aesthetic approach to life and, as typical Enlightenment Man, he was familiar with philosophy and letters and moved easily in intellectual circles. He first visited Italy in 1736 and studied painting in Rome and Naples, where he acquired the disciplined facility of drawing which was the underpinning strength of his work. From somewhat ornate baroque beginnings he gradually developed a distinctive style notable for its simplicity and directness.

THE CONTEMPORARY VIEW

Truth is the leading and inseparable principle in all works of art. . .
beauty lies in naturalness, in the real representation of truth, and
the real existence of things.

Allan Ramsay, *Dialogue on Taste (1755)*

I love Ramsay. You will not find a man in whose conversation there
is more instruction, more information, and more elegance, than in
Ramsay's.

Samuel Johnson quoted in Boswell's *Life* (1778)

THE WIDER VIEW

Ramsay's paintings are, simultaneously, striking examples of the social art of portraiture and of the individuality of the artist's vision. Through his canvases a picture of the age emerges. The nobility of Scotland, such as the Duke of Argyll, sat for Ramsay, as did George III, when Prince of Wales, but so too did humbler gentry and worthies. Until recently Joshua Reynolds' reputation was the greater, but it has increasingly been recognised that with Ramsay the Scots tradition of painting was established and the cultural strand of the Enlightenment begun. Another Scot with an international reputation, Henry Raeburn *(q.v.)*, was to inherit and build upon all this.

NEW LANARK COTTON MILLS

In its long (1785-1968) history of uninterrupted production, the cotton spinning mills at what David Dale, its creator, called New Lanark, on the River Clyde, became a mecca for industrialists, educationists and, in later years, historians and sociologists. From its inception, Dale, a Glasgow banker, intended that the workers and inhabitants of the mills and the linked community would benefit from systematic provision of planned working conditions and services such as schools and housing of a high standard. Child labour was employed, as was the norm, but there was an unheard-of concern for safety. It was fortunate that Dale's successor as manager in 1800 was a man of the same stamp as a leader, but with an even greater interest in social engineering. Under Robert Owen, New Lanark became a show-place for experiments in social harmony, with a particular emphasis on education – the Institute for the Formation of Character being an early example of adult education.

THE CONTEMPORARY VIEW

The first of the mills erected was 154 feet in length. . . a tunnel nearly 100 yards in length was cut through a rocky hill, to form a passage for the water of the Clyde, by which it was propelled. . . About 1200 persons are employed. . . many are children, for whose comfort the company have made every requisite provision
Lewis's *Topographical Dictionary of Scotland* (1846)

THE WIDER VIEW

As his many visitors observed, Owen was successful in combining philanthropy with business acumen – New Lanark gave him a personal fortune. His later social experiments in America were less successful, however. Curiously, some of the same kind of vigour and imagination displayed by the pioneers is currently being employed by those responsible for New Lanark in its Third Age, as a World Heritage Site.

THE PUBLICATION OF THE KILMARNOCK EDITION

This, the famous edition of *Poems Chiefly in the Scottish Dialect* by Robert Burns, was published by John Wilson of Kilmarnock on 31 July, when 612 copies were printed. Its success among all classes of society was almost instantaneous – eager crowds of sucbscribers crowded to the Star Inn Close in Kilmarnock to buy, as quickly as "Wee Johnnie" Wilson's folders, stitchers and binders could produce the thin octavo volumes. Much of the success was due to the enthusiasm of the poet's dedicated supporters like Gavin Hamilton and Robert Aitken, who purchased the poems in large numbers.

As is well known today, the edition contained only some of the works which won Burns "undying fame". It made, however, a sensation which catapulted its author onto a national stage; within weeks the poems had sold out and the announcement of an Edinburgh edition was a fitting accompaniment to the poet's triumphal arrival in the capital's literary salons. Burns's reputation was at the greatest height it was to attain in his lifetime.

THE CONTEMPORARY VIEW

Though a Rhymer from his [i.e. the author's] *earliest years. . . it was not until very lately, that the applause, perhaps the partiality of Friendship, wakened his vanity so far as to make him think any thing of his was worth showing; and none of the following works were ever composed with a view to the press.*

From Burns's Preface to the Kilmarnock edition

His observations on human characters are acute and sagacious, and his descriptions are lively and just. Of rustic peasantry he has a rich fund, and some of his softer scenes are touched with inimitable delicacy. He seems to be a boon companion, and often startles us with a dash of libertinism which will keep some readers at a distance.

From a review of the poems in *The Edinburgh Magazine*

I can well remember how that even ploughboys and maidservants would have gladly bestowed the wages which they earned the most hardly, and which they wanted for necessary clothing, if they might but procure the works of Burns.

Heron's *Memoir of Burns*

I had taken the last farewell of my few friends; my chest was on the road
to Greenock; I had composed the last song that I should ever measure
in Caledonia, when Dr. Blacklock's opinion that I would meet with
encouragement in Edinburgh for a second edition, fired me so much,
that I posted away for that city.

Burns's *Autobiography*

THE WIDER VIEW

In the life of Scotland's bard this event occurred in rather melodramatic circumstances. On the eve of his success he had written to a friend: "My hour is now come; you and I shall never meet in Britain more." In the corner was the sea-chest with his belongings, ready for emigration to Jamaica. In his Autobiographical Letters he wrote, "I was pretty sure my poems would meet with some applause; but at the worst, the roar of the Atlantic would deafen the voice of Censure, and the novelty of West-Indian scenes make me forget Neglect." Burns did not at first realise it, but the gradually swelling chorus of approval would keep him on his native soil. Success, even if impermanent, had arrived; happiness was less certain.

The best-laid schemes o' Mice an' Men
Gang aft agely,
An' lea' e us nocht but grief an pain,
For promis'd joy!

Still thou art blest, compar'd wi' me!
The present only toucheth thee:
But och! I backward cast my e'e,
On prospects drear!
An' forward, tho' I canna see'
I guess an' fear!

"To a Mouse"

THE OPENING OF THE
FORTH AND CLYDE CANAL

The narrow neck of land between the Clyde and the Forth had attracted strategists from Roman times. A canal across central Scotland was an obvious development and had been proposed in the seventeenth century. In March 1768 the Yorkshire engineer John Smeaton, who had been engaged to survey the route for the promoters, was appointed as Engineer. Glaswegian fears that the chosen route, from Grangemouth to Bowling on the Clyde, 10 miles downstream from Glasgow, would bypass the city and harm their trade were allayed by the decision to include a branch canal into Glasgow.

Construction started in June 1768 at Grangemouth and in 1773 the first traffic appeared on the canal, which was then operational as far as Kirkintilloch. Completion of the "Great Canal" came in the summer of 1790 when all 38.75 miles of the canal and 39 locks were finished at an estimated cost of £330,000.

THE CONTEMPORARY VIEW

On the arrival of the vessel at Bowling Bay. . . the ceremony of of the junction of the Forth and Clyde was performed. . . by Archibald Spiers Esq. of Elderslie, chairman of the committee of management, who. . . launched a hogshead of water of the river Forth into the Clyde as a symbol of joining the eastern and western seas together.
Scots Magazine, Report of opening in July 1790

THE WIDER VIEW

The Forth and Clyde was Britain's first sea-to-sea canal. Sea-going vessels could pass from coast to coast without expensive transhipment of cargoes. It also linked important industrial centres such as the Carron Works near Falkirk and an extensive internal and export trade in minerals, agricultural produce and manufactured goods was developed. The canal also offered the easiest passenger route from Glasgow and the west to Edinburgh and the east.

THE PUBLICATION OF THE
FIRST STATISTICAL ACCOUNT

Sir John Sinclair of Ulbster had a passion for improvement and progress which manifested itself on his Caithness estate. He also had a considerable degree of political influence and well developed persuasive powers. These all came together in his massive scheme to organise a complete survey of Scotland, a description of every parish in the Kingdom, drawn up by the resident clergyman of the established Church.

The term "statistical account" perhaps gives us today a misleading and limited impression of the scope of this survey, published in 21 volumes between 1791 and 1798. The parish accounts vary considerably, some being fairly terse responses to Sinclair's questionnaire, others give detailed histories, analyses of landholdings, topographical information and sociological statistics.

As a reward for the clergy's involvement, Sinclair persuaded the Government to provide funds for the support of their families and procured parliamentary grants for less well-endowed parishes. Sinclair's later analysis of the Account was appropriately dedicated to the Clergy of the Church of Scotland in recognition of their "patriotic labours, to ascertain the circumstances of their native country".

THE CONTEMPORARY VIEW

A statistical account in Sinclair's view was
an enquiry into the state of a country for the purpose of ascertaining the quantum of happiness enjoyed by its inhabitants and means of its future improvement.

THE WIDER VIEW

Sinclair's work, which he repeated in the 1820s, not only produced an invaluable tool for development and social study but one of the key Scottish historical documents, surveying the country at critical moments in the agricultural and industrial revolutions. By providing an overview of Scotland from Unst to Wigtown, it also played a significant part in breaking down internal barriers and created the possibility of more effective Government intervention in social problems.

THE TRIAL OF THOMAS MUIR

On 30 August 1793 Thomas Muir stood trial for sedition. Muir, an advocate, came from a middle-class family whose estate in Bishopbriggs gave him the territorial designation of "Muir of Huntershill" by which he is commonly known.

Muir held radical views and had been involved in religious controversies and the reform movements of the 1790s. Muir's "sedition" consisted in advocating a wider franchise, frequent Parliamentary elections, municipal reform and, perhaps most alarmingly, carrying out political activity among the working classes. The presiding judge, Lord Braxfield (the model for Stevenson's *Weir of Hermiston*), was determined on a conviction and the jury was packed with known Government supporters. Muir, perhaps unwisely, defended himself. He was found guilty and sentenced to transportation for 14 years.

THE CONTEMPORARY VIEW

*I have devoted myself to the cause of the people. It is a good cause
– it shall ultimately prevail*

From Muir's final speech

Government. . . in this country is made up of the landed interest, which alone has a right to be represented; as for the rabble. . . what hold has the nation of them?

From Lord Braxfield's summing up

THE WIDER VIEW

The Scottish radicals were inspired by Revolutionary France and the overthrow of the *ancien régime*. Although Muir repudiated violence, events in France had moved on from the heady days of 1789 and the fall of the Bastille to the execution of Louis XVI in January 1793. War had broken out between Britain and France in 1792. Muir's activities and his connections with France awoke the worst instincts of a frightened Scottish establishment presided over by Henry Dundas. Muir's sentence was exceptionally severe because as a landowner and professional man he was seen as a greater threat than the radical weavers he associated with.

THE DEATH OF JAMES HUTTON

The son of an Edinburgh merchant, James Hutton trained as a doctor in Edinburgh, Paris and Leiden before turning to scientific studies. Although perhaps one of the lesser-known figures of the Scottish Enlightenment, he assumes tremendous significance within his own field of geology. The claim can be made with ample justification that Hutton created and founded the scientific study of the earth and its rocks when, in 1785, he completed his lifelong task and published the *Theory of the Earth*. In this paper he brought together his musings on years spent working and studying the land as a farmer in the Borders and travelling in England and Europe. By applying scientific inductive reasoning, Hutton was able to put forward a single unified theory about the earth, "this terrestrial system", its origins and construction, much of which remains acceptable today. In particular, by arguing for an immense revision of the timescale for these processes, Hutton prepared the ground for Darwin's ideas.

THE CONTEMPORARY VIEW

The heights of our land are thus levelled with the shores; our fertile plains are formed from the ruins of the mountains; and those travelling materials are still pursued by the moving water, and propelled along the inclined surface of the earth.

James Hutton, *Theory of the Earth*

THE WIDER VIEW

Hutton's ideas were a shock to beliefs about the origins of the universe which supposed that the earth had been created on a particular day in 4004 B.C. For some peculiar Scottish reason, however, he escaped being anathematised, and indeed lived to see a general acceptance of his work and of the science he originated. Typical of his age in his breadth of interests, he edited his close friend Adam Smith's *Essays on Philosphical Subjects* in 1795.

1803

THE APPOINTMENT OF COMMISSIONERS FOR HIGHLAND ROADS AND BRIDGES

General Wade's road-building *(q.v.)* had continued under military auspices throughout the eighteenth century. With the Jacobite threat ended an economical Government increasingly resented the army building and maintaining roads for civilian use.

In 1802 the Government commissioned Thomas Telford (1757-1834) to report on the condition and communications of the Highlands. Telford's plans envisaged a road system designed for economic, as opposed to strategic needs. In 1803 a Commission for Highland Roads and Bridges was established, with Telford as engineer, to carry through these recommendations. Funding for roads and bridges came in equal measure from Government and local landowners. The Commission's powers were wide, even later extending to the erection of churches and manses.

Another commission was established, again with Telford as engineer, to construct the Caledonian Canal on a 60 mile long route through the Great Glen.

THE CONTEMPORARY VIEW

I consider these improvements among the greatest blessings ever conferred on any country. About two hundred thousand pounds has been granted in fifteen years. It has been the means of advancing the country at least a century.

Thomas Telford on Roads and Bridges

THE WIDER VIEW

Telford's eighteen years as engineer saw 920 miles of roads constructed and 280 miles of military road remade. Of the 1,200 bridges, including the first one built – that over the Tay at Dunkeld – many are still part of our road network. The Caledonian Canal, commenced in 1804, was partly motivated by the need to move warships from coast to coast. It was not completed until 1822, at a cost of £800,000, when the wartime strategic necessity had gone. Designed in the age of sail, the first commercial voyage from the "Western to the Eastern Sea", in November 1822, was by Henry Bell's steam-boat *Comet II*.

THE SUTHERLAND CLEARANCES

Few subjects are as emotive as the Clearances. The estate most popularly vilified is that of the Countess of Sutherland and the name most execrated, Patrick Sellar, who heartlessly cleared Strathnaver in 1814. The Sutherland estates had commenced the clearances of Farr and Lairg in 1807 but the process started earlier and continued to mid-century throughout much of the Highlands.

Two forms of Clearance existed; the encouragement of migration to the Lowlands and overseas, a noted example of this being the Earl of Selkirk's settlements in Canada and secondly the forcible eviction of tenants from potential sheep-grazing lands.

THE CONTEMPORARY VIEW

. . . last year when a ship sailed from Portree for America, the people on shore were almost distracted when they saw their relatives go off. . . This year there was not a tear shed. The people on shore seemed to think that they would soon follow. This indifference is a mortal sign for the country.
James Boswell, *Journal of a Tour to the Hebrides* (1786)

THE WIDER VIEW

A clan chief's status had depended on the number of his fighting men. Highland society had involved a patriarchal assumption of responsibility for the clanspeople. The post-1745 order introduced a cash economy to the Highlands and abolished the chief's traditional role. A simultaneous sharp population rise occurred – Mull's population rose from 10,000 in 1755 to 18,000 in 1811. Agriculture in the Highlands was marginal, industry was insignificant; kelp gathering for use in chemical processes had boomed during the Napoleonic wars but the renewed importation of barilla, following victory in Spain, destroyed the kelp market. The situation was made for inevitable tragedy. Some landlords ineffectually tried to help, others saw sheep-grazing as their only recourse and implemented brutal clearances, depopulating large areas.

LACHLAN MACQUARIE APPOINTED AS GOVERNOR OF NEW SOUTH WALES

Born in 1762 into a chiefly family in the island of Ulva off Mull, Lachlan Macquarie had a varied military career in America, Egypt and India before being posted to New South Wales in command of the 73rd Regiment (The Perthshire Regiment) to accompany a new Governor appointed to replace William Bligh, of "Bounty" notoriety, who had been the cause of a rebellion. Ill health forced the resignation of the newly appointed Governor before he could sail and Macquarie applied for and received the post.

In an enlightened and energetic 12-year-long governorship Macquarie saw New South Wales's prosperity greatly increased, its population trebled and a humane policy extended to both Aborigines and freed convicts. His desire to integrate ex-convicts into the life of the colony enraged immigrant settlers and critics in London and resulted in political moves which led to his resignation in 1821.

THE CONTEMPORARY VIEW

The Great Objects of attention are to improve the Morals of the Colonists, to encourage Marriage, to provide for Education, to prohibit the use of Spiritous Liquors, to increase the Agriculture. . .
Macquarie's Colonial Office Instructions, 1809

THE WIDER VIEW

Often described as the "Father of Australia", Macquarie was not the first Scottish Governor; Captain John Hunter R.N., from Leith, had sailed with the "First Fleet", the original convict shipment to Botany Bay in 1787 and in 1795 became the Colony's second Governor. Macquarie's successor was another Scottish soldier, Sir Thomas Brisbane from Largs.

Scots played a significant part in Australia's development, involuntarily as convicts like the 1820 Radicals *(q.v.)*, but also as free settlers, miners, agriculturalists, ministers, soldiers and explorers like John McDouall Stuart from Dysart, whose epic journeys between 1859 and 1862 charted the continent's vast unknown interior.

COMET – EUROPE'S FIRST COMMERCIAL STEAMSHIP

In August 1812 the 42 foot steamship *Comet* sailed down the Clyde under the power of "air, wind and steam". *Comet* was not Scotland's first steam boat; the *Charlotte Dundas* had run trials on the Forth and Clyde Canal some years earlier and in 1788 Patrick Millar of Dalswinton had experimented with a steam ship. *Comet*, however launched Europe's first commercial steamer service.

Henry Bell, the *Comet's* designer and owner, had succeeded where many others had failed. Building on established technology and utilising local shipbuilding and engineering skills, *Comet* pioneered practical steam navigation and was soon followed on to the Clyde and other rivers by larger and faster vessels. The Clyde became an internationally recognised centre of shipbuilding and engineering.

Bell was born at Torphichen, West Lothian, in 1767 and trained as a millwright. He later was in business as a builder and engineer in Glasgow. By 1812 he was well-established as a hotelier in the newly-established Clyde resort of Helensburgh and *Comet* was, in part at least, designed to bring guests comfortably and reliably down to take the waters at the Baths Inn.

Bell's engineering skill and entrepreneurial flair failed to find its just reward, partly due to his financial improvidence. He died in comparative poverty in 1830.

THE CONTEMPORARY VIEW

Brunel, one of the greatest engineers of the age, commented:
Bell did what we engineers all failed in – he gave us the sea steamer; his scheming was Britain's steaming.

THE WIDER VIEW

Robert Fulton started the world's first steamship service on the Hudson River, New York State, in 1807. Fulton had earlier visited Britain and, along with Bell, inspected the *Charlotte Dundas*, laid up on the Forth and Clyde Canal and talked to her designer, William Symington.

"WAVERLEY; OR 'TIS SIXTY YEARS SINCE"

The publication of yet another three volume novel by the Edinburgh publishing house of Constable might seem an unremarkable event, even if the first edition sold out in five weeks. However this novel was to affect literary tastes and fashions for generations and influence the way that the world looked at Scotland and Scotland looked at herself.

No author's name appeared on the title page. Although the identity of "the author of *Waverley*" or "the great Unknown" was never really a great mystery, a formal elucidation did not appear until 1827.

The "author of *Waverley*" virtually created the historical novel and his series of novels on Scottish themes gave full play to his antiquarian and historical tastes and allowed scope for the expression of his sentimental conservatism and love for an older and fast-changing Scotland.

Walter Scott, advocate, Sheriff-Depute of Selkirk and Clerk of the Court of Session was the "great Unknown". His literary reputation was second to none in early nineteenth century Britain. Scott refused the Poet Laureateship in 1813 but the baronetcy he received in 1820 fittingly recognised his literary pre-eminence.

THE CONTEMPORARY VIEW

. . . a work decidedly original, and possessing strong claims to public attention. Report assigns it to the most admired poet of the age. . . and we see no reason that even such a writer could have to disown a performance like the present.

Scots Magazine: Review, July 1814

THE WIDER VIEW

Scott's writings created an international image for Scotland, popularising it as a romantic land peopled by heroes and villains. His books, which had a global readership, stimulated tourism, particularly to the Trossachs area, the setting of much of the action of *Waverley, Rob Roy* and his earlier narrative poem *The Lady of the Lake*.

LAUNCH OF *BLACKWOOD'S MAGAZINE*

Blackwood's Edinburgh Monthly Magazine, was one of the publishing phenomena of the nineteenth century. Founded by William Blackwood, an Edinburgh bookseller, it provided a home for the writings of authors such as John Galt, James Hogg "the Ettrick Shepherd" and a group of writers who became known as the "Blackwood Group" – including J.G. Lockhart (Walter Scott's son-in-law), John Wilson ("Christopher North") and David Macbeth Moir, who wrote under the pen name of "Delta". The politics of *Blackwood's* was Tory and one of the motives behind its launch was to oppose the Whig *Edinburgh Review*.

THE CONTEMPORARY VIEW

Already. . . the state of literature in Scotland had assumed somewhat of a new phasis. . . Mr Blackwood and his Magazine had attained nearly the zenith of their prosperity, and volunteer contributions. . . showered upon him, from all quarters. Among his new allies, John Galt, held a distinguished place; having, doubtless, exhibited a notable vein of originality, inasmuch as he contrived, by a quaint style of eccentric naïveté to render even the merest platitudes diverting.

Robert Pearse Gillies, *Memoirs of a Literary Veteran*

THE WIDER VIEW

Blackwood's initial strength and vitality, derived from contributors like Galt and Hogg, rather declined and a self-consciously pawky Scots humour came to dominate. However *Blackwood's Magazine* was a major force in nineteenth-century British publishing, well chronicled by the novelist Margaret Oliphant, and did much to ensure the survival of Scots as a literary language alongside English. It was in *Blackwood's* in 1829 that the haunting lines of the "Canadian Boat Song" first appeared, anonymously, but probably by David MacBeth Moir.

From the lone shieling of the misty island
Mountains divide us, and the waste of seas –
Yet still the blood is strong, the heart is Highland
And we in dreams behold the Hebrides.

"THE RADICAL WAR"

Post-Napoleonic War economic depression fuelled agitation for political reform. Industrialisation's effects bore hard on workers such as handloom weavers and an unsettling mixture of political and economic grievances was at work. Lord Liverpool's Tory Government, fearing a working class rising, employed spies and *agents provocateurs* to penetrate the reform movement.

Numerous mass reform meetings were held during 1819 and in February 1820 members of a radical committee were arrested on suspicion of planning insurrection. In April 60,000 workers answered a strike call in the west of Scotland, placards announcing a provisional government appeared in Glasgow and Paisley and some forty radicals marched on the Carron Ironworks *(q.v.)* hoping to seize armaments. They were reinforced by a group from Stirling but in a clash at Bonnymuir were easily overcome by troops. Three leaders, Hardie, Baird and Wilson were executed for treason, 19 others suffered transportation.

THE CONTEMPORARY VIEW

Scotland free or a desart
"Radical War" banner slogan

The perfect facility with which a party of forty or fifty thousand weavers could march from Glasgow, and seize upon the Banks and the Castle of Edinburgh without ever being heard of till they appeared in our streets was demonstrated. Our magistrates therefore invited all loyal citizens to congregate, with such arms as they had, at various assigned posts. I repaired to the Assembly rooms in George Street, with a stick. . .

Henry Thomas Cockburn, *Diaries*

THE WIDER VIEW

The "Radical War" followed Manchester's Peterloo Massacre of August 1819 and awoke memories of Thomas Muir's trial in 1793 *(q.v.)* The insurrection's nationalistic and republican character has been hotly, if inconclusively, debated. The insurrectionists gained martyrs places in Scottish folklore. Radical sentiment, whatever its motivation or scale, as Cockburn's exaggerated account suggests, greatly alarmed the establishment.

KING GEORGE IV VISITS SCOTLAND

After James VI moved south in 1603 *(q.v.)* he and his successors paid increasingly scant attention to Scotland. James returned once in 1617, his son Charles I, born in Dunfermline, was crowned at Edinburgh in 1633 *(q.v.)*. Charles II was crowned in Scotland in 1651 and although his brother, later James VII and II, was much in Scotland as Duke of York, visits by reigning monarchs ended with Charles II.

Internal unrest and 60 years of Jacobite threat made royal visits impolitic. By the 1820s all this was safely past and Sir Walter Scott turned his mind to bringing George IV, who had come to the throne in 1820, on a visit to Scotland. The King came north by sea for a hectic fortnight, landing at Leith on 14 August. Holyrood Palace, lacking regular royal use since the days of the Duke of York, was used for the state occasions although the King stayed at the Duke of Buccleuch's Dalkeith Palace.

THE CONTEMPORARY VIEW

We are satisfied that we have seen our Sovereign, and that he has seen us; we flatter ourselves that both parties will be the better for this knowledge of each other.

                                        Scots Magazine, August 1822

THE WIDER VIEW

George IV threw himself into the spirit of the visit; whisky, tartan, presbyterian service at the High Kirk of St Giles and all. The trip cemented post-Jacobite reconciliation, boosted the popularity of an unpopular King and created a taste for an *ersatz* tartanry which has since irritated some sensitive Scots. Sir Walter revelled in the visit's success, during which he arranged the return of Mons Meg to the ramparts of Edinburgh Castle and, important to one driven by his mixture of romantic Toryism and nationalist sentiment, got the peerages forfeited in the Jacobite rebellion restored.

THE DEATH OF SIR HENRY RAEBURN

The death on 8 July 1823 of Henry Raeburn, newly appointed King's Limner in Scotland, removed the leading Scottish artist of his generation. For over thirty years his portraits had delineated Scottish society. Technique and insight combined to produce a series of portraits which now seem to define his age. Portraits of men of power – the judge Lord Braxfield, of writers like Scott, of landed society – Alasdair Macdonnell of Glengarry, are matched by gentler depictions of women – Janet Dundas or Mrs Gregory and by idiosyncratic works such as the portrait of the Rev. Robert Walker skating on Duddingston Loch.

Born in 1756, apprenticed to a goldsmith, he first practised as a miniature painter before following the tradition of a study tour to Rome. Back in Scotland by 1787 he built up a large practice. Raeburn combined the tradition of naturalness and observation exemplified by earlier Scottish painters such as Ramsay with something of the grand manner of his English contemporary, Joshua Reynolds. His best works combine informality and naturalness with acute psychological perception – as evidenced in his last portrait of Sir Walter Scott. Raeburn was knighted by George IV on his Royal Visit to Scotland in 1822 *(q.v.)*

THE CONTEMPORARY VIEW

There was nothing elaborate about his best portraits. . . By a few bold and skilfully managed touches he produced striking effects.
Cumberland Hill, *History and Reminiscences of Stockbridge* (1874)

THE WIDER VIEW

In 1810 Raeburn contemplated moving to London but in fact spent all his working life in Scotland, a decision which did not prevent his gaining an international reputation. Raeburn's empirical approach to portraiture was in keeping with contemporary Scottish philosophical principles of common sense enunciated by scholars such as Thomas Reid, the subject of one of Raeburn's finest portraits.

THE DEATH OF LORD BYRON

The death, from rheumatic fever in Greece, of the sixth Baron Byron of Newstead Abbey, Nottingham, ended a short, scandal-filled life of 36 years, a life apparently unlikely to feature in this work. However Byron in *Don Juan* staked his claim to inclusion:

But I am half a Scot by birth, and bred
A whole one. . .

His mother was an Aberdeenshire Gordon and returned home when George Gordon Noel Byron was four. He was educated at Aberdeen Grammar School and paid regular visits to his Gordon relatives. Succeeding to the family title at ten, he left Scotland forever, though never deserting it emotionally.

However when his early work *Hours of Idleness* was attacked in the Edinburgh Review his romantic nationalism did not impede the compostion of his riposte *English Bards and Scotch Reviewers*. International fame came with the publication of *Childe Harold's Pilgrimage* in 1812, when he noted:"I awoke one morning and found myself famous." Notoriety followed an affair with Lady Caroline Lamb and a rumoured incestuous relationship with his half-sister. Scandal forced him into exile in 1816. In 1823 he became involved in the Greek independence struggle.

THE CONTEMPORARY VIEW

England! thy beauties are tame and domestic
To one who has roved o'er the mountains afar:
Oh for the crags that are wild and majestic!
The steep frowning glories of dark Loch na Garr.
                    Byron, *"Lachin y Gair"*

THE WIDER VIEW

The ultra-respectable Walter Scott *(q.v.)* might seem an unlikely figure to win the sympathy of Byron the scandalous Romantic, yet Byron wrote:

With his politics I have nothing to do, they differ from mine. . . I say
that Walter Scott is as nearly a thorough good man as man can be. . .
                    Byron to Stendhal, May 1823

THE OPENING OF THE MONKLAND AND KIRKINTILLOCH RAILWAY

The rich coalfields around Glasgow contributed to many transport developments such as the Forth and Clyde Canal *(q.v.)*. The desire by local landowners and coalmasters to link the Monklands pits with the Glasgow and Edinburgh markets and to establish an export route through the Clyde and Forth ports lay behind the building of a 10-mile long railway from Airdrie to the canal at Kirkintilloch. Parliamentary approval was granted in May 1824 and construction started in June with part of the line being open to traffic in May 1826.

The line, using Birkinshaw's patent malleable iron rails, was Scotland's first railway, as opposed to tramways or plateways, and came just a year after the pioneering Stockton and Darlington Railway. Early traffic on the Monkland and Kirkintilloch was horse-drawn but use of the strong edge rails rather than cast iron plates meant that locomotive traction was a possible option and in May 1831 the first locomotive, imaginatively titled *No. 1*, was placed on the line, becoming Scotland's first commercially successful steam locomotive.

THE CONTEMPORARY VIEW

The Gartsheary Coal (from the Monkland Coal-Field) is now introduced for the first time into Edinburgh, in consequence of the opening of the Kirkintilloch Railway. . .

Coal-merchant's advertisement, June 1826

. . . it (Locomotive No.1.) *passed several miles along the Railway, sometimes going at the rate of fifteen miles per hour. . .*

Glasgow Courier, 12 May 1831

THE WIDER VIEW

The opening of the Monkland and Kirkintilloch Railway proved to be of the greatest assistance to local coal-mining and to the development of the important iron industry around Glasgow. The line's first locomotive, built by Murdoch & Aitken in Glasgow, was the precursor of countless Glasgow-built locomotives and the origins of one of the city's most famous and important, though now vanished, industries.

JAMES BEAUMONT NEILSON PATENTS THE HOT-BLAST PROCESS

The Carron Works *(q.v.)* had introduced coke-smelting of iron ore to Scotland. The next stage in the development of Scotland's iron industry was the identification of the black-band ironstone deposits around Glasgow as a potential ore by David Mushet (1772–1847). This stone differs from the clayband ores used at Carron, in that it itself contains sufficient coal to be its own fuel in the refining process.

The invention of the hot-blast allowed the exploitation of the black-band ironstone. Neilson (1792–1865), a Glasgow-born engineer, reasoned that if the flow of air into the iron-making furnaces could be heated before use then this would dry the air and increase the action of the oxygen. Previously iron-makers had believed that cool air was desirable and had introduced refrigerating plant to achieve this. Neilson's 1828 Patent made it possible to reduce production costs significantly and increase output besides making possible the use of the black-band ore.

Neilson's process was quickly adopted but the royalty of one shilling per ton on iron produced by his process was resisted by an influential group of ironmasters who initiated a five year long legal campaign to overturn his Patent. This ended with the House of Lords finding in Neilson's favour.

THE CONTEMPORARY VIEW

Notwithstanding. . . the losses from litigation, the inventor of the hot-blast realised a moderate fortune; and it may be estimated that his country benefitted by his invention to the extent of about twelve millions per annum. . .

Thomson, *Biographical Dictionary of Famous Scotsmen* (1870)

THE WIDER VIEW

Mushet and Neilson's work came at a time of rapidly growing demand for pig iron by the rapidly expanding railway, shipbuilding and engineering industries. Between 1830 and 1835 Scottish iron production doubled due to the use of the black-band ironstone.

THE FIRST REFORM ACT

Before the 1832 Reform Act the Scottish Parliamentary electorate was around 5,000 adult males. The opportunities such a tiny electorate presented for corruption and manipulation were obvious and had been skilfully used by Government managers like Henry Dundas. Similarly, in England, the corruption of "rotten boroughs" was notorious, providing the theme for John Galt's novel of 1832 *The Member*.

Reform agitation had been endemic from Thomas Muir's era *(q.v.)* through the French wars to the "Radical War" of 1820 *(q.v.)*. The Whig party, coming to power in 1830, supported the extension of political rights to the middle class.

The Act raised Scotland's Westminster representation from 45 to 53 seats, and extended the franchise to over 60,000 voters – householders of £10 value in the burghs and property owners of £10 or tenants of £50 rental in the county seats. Growing towns like Paisley were now represented.

THE CONTEMPORARY VIEW

6th August 1832. The regeneration of Scotland is now secured. Our Reform Bill has become law. . . Nobody who did not see it could believe the orderly joy with which the people have received their emancipation, or the judgement with which they seem inclined to use it.

Henry Cockburn, *Diaries*

. . . my wisest course was to make the best bargain I could for the borough, and retire. . . well aware that the one-and-twenty millions and a half will not be long content with such a fractional representation as it is proposed to give them. . .

John Galt, *The Member* (1832)

THE WIDER VIEW

The 1832 Act was indeed a modest measure, hence the outbreak of Chartist agitation in 1838. Much radical energy in Scotland went into church politics in the years leading to the Disruption *(q.v.)* of 1843. In 1868 a second Reform Act gave male householder franchise in urban areas.

"THE FATHER OF CLYDE SHIPBUILDING" FOUNDS HIS SHIPYARD

When in 1841 Robert Napier founded a shipyard at Govan on the Clyde he was already one of Glasgow's leading engineers, the highlight of his pre-1841 career being the contract for the first ships for the Cunard line. Napier had provided the engines and much of the inspiration for these four wooden ships. However wooden shipbuilding was reaching its limits and Napier decided to create a new iron shipbuilding yard; from it and its succesors came some of the finest ships of the age and a stream of pioneering shipbuilders and engineers who established the Clyde's pre-eminence and won Napier the title of "The Father of Clyde Shipbuilding".

Among Napier's "firsts" at Govan were the Royal Navy's first iron warships *Jackal*, *Lizard* and *Bloodhound* and the world's first train ferry, the *Leviathan* of 1849. When the Cunarder *Persia* was launched in 1855 she was the world's largest ship and perhaps the most beautiful ship of her age.

Born into a Dumbarton family of engineers, Napier was apprenticed to his father before setting up in business in 1815. His first marine engine, for the *Leven* steamer of 1823, still survives in his native town, a fitting tribute to his workmanship and his part in the Clyde's story.

THE CONTEMPORARY VIEW

Sir James Melvill of the East India Company described Napier as:
. . . the man who. . . has given practical effect to the inventions of Watt, and has passed to the world the great blessings of steam navigation.

THE WIDER VIEW

Although the Clyde pioneered the steam-ship, the centre of shipbuilding activity had moved south and it was largely due to Napier that the Clyde regained its ascendancy and became the major commercial and naval shipbuilding area in the mid and later nineteenth century.

THE DISRUPTION

In Scottish presbyterianism's complex history of disputes and secessions one event stands out as "The Disruption" – the departure of one third of the established Church of Scotland to form the Free Church of Scotland. A struggle had raged over the relationship between Church and State. One critical battlefield was over a congregation's right to choose its own minister rather than have one appointed by the landowning heritors. The 1834 General Assembly passed the Veto Act empowering congregations to reject such presentations, an Act declared unlawful by the Court of Session and the House of Lords. The increasingly powerful Evangelical faction within the Church felt that these decisions undermined the Kirk's claim to spiritual independence and sought this in a new Church. The defining moment came on 18 May 1843 at the General Assemby when the dissidents tabled a protest and marched out.

The Free Church swiftly established a parallel national structure of churches (500 built in the first year), schools and foreign missions. The 474 ministers who left the Auld Kirk at the Disruption surrendered their social position, security, manses, and stipends and became solely dependent on congregational giving.

THE CONTEMPORARY VIEW

The wee Kirk, the free Kirk,
The Kirk wi'out the steeple.
The auld Kirk, the cauld Kirk,
The Kirk wi'out the people.
Contemporary jingle

. . . a noble and heart-stirring spectacle
W.E. Gladstone

THE WIDER VIEW

The 1840s were a troubled decade; Chartism in Britain, the Revolutions of 1848 in France, Italy and the Austro-Hungarian Empire. The Disruption of 1843, though lacking the violence of the continental manifestations, reflected this widespread unrest and similarly divided families and communities.

1846

WILLIAM THOMSON APPOINTED PROFESSOR OF NATURAL PHILOSOPHY AT GLASGOW UNIVERSITY

Thomson was born in Belfast but his brilliant career was identified with Glasgow, the city of his adoption. Brought to Glasgow, his mother's birthplace, when his father was appointed Professor of Mathematics there in 1832, he entered its University at the age of 11, went to Cambridge six years later and returned, via Paris, to take up a professorial chair at Glasgow at the age of 22.

Thomson's work on mathematical physics led to his framing his two laws of thermodynamics. Later he turned to electricity and magnetism. Thomson was showered with honours and awards, a Fellow of the Royal Society at 27, knighted in 1866, created Baron Kelvin in 1892 and received the newly-created Order of Merit in 1902. He died in 1907 and was buried in Westminster Abbey.

THE CONTEMPORARY VIEW

In 1896 Kelvin celebrated his professorial jubilee. Congratulatory addresses were received from around the world. Balliol College, Oxford's address is representative:

The long and brilliant career of discovery which has placed you in the front rank of the scientific men of this century it is needless for us to attempt to describe, but we venture to refer to one remarkable and almost unique characteristic of it – namely, that it has been equally distinguished for the profundity and originality of its achievements in the field of abstract mathematical and physical science, and for the ingenuity and inventive power with which the principles of science have been turned to practical use. . .

THE WIDER VIEW

Kelvin was indeed distinguished by a commitment to the practical application of science. He was closely and practically involved in the laying of the first successful transatlantic telegraph cable (the achievement which won him his knighthood) and he established a company to manufacture his many inventions.

SIMPSON INTRODUCES CHLOROFORM

James Young Simpson (1811-1870), one of a number of Scots who made striking contributions to the rise of scientific medicine, was a product of the Edinburgh medical school, which was at the pinnacle of its fame in the early years of Victoria's reign. Born, the son of a baker, in Bathgate, West Lothian, he was responsible for many advances in obstetrics, but is best known as a pioneer of the controlled use of anaesthetics in surgery.

In childbirth and in other operations there was much pain and suffering and no adequate way of dealing with them, until experiments with the use of ether were conducted in the USA in the 1840s. Simpson and his assistants experimented with ether and then with chloroform, first on themselves and then in obstetrics at the Edinburgh Royal Infirmary in 1847.

THE CONTEMPORARY VIEW

[Use] *of chloroform in labour. . . [was] contrary to the sound principles of physiology and morality. 'In sorrow shalt thou bring forth children', was an established law of nature – an ordinance of the Almighty, as stated in the Bible. . . There could not be a doubt that it was a most unnatural practice to destroy the consciousness of women during labour, the pains and sorrows of which exerted a most powerful and salutory influence upon their religious and moral character. . .*

Dr. Robert Lee, *The Lancet* 24 December 1853

THE WIDER VIEW

Initially there was much opposition to Simpson's work, but the practices he advocated were boosted by Queen Victoria, who appointed him Physician to the Queen in Scotland and who was anaesthetised during the birth of her eighth child, Prince Leopold, in 1853. In 1866 he was created a baronet, the first such distinction given to a doctor practising in Scotland.

1848

ANDREW CARNEGIE
EMIGRATES TO USA

Born in Dunfermline, the son of a linen weaver, Carnegie was the epitome of the self-made man. From a radical Chartist background he became a millionaire and founded a new kind of principled philanthropy. Emigrating to Pennsylvania in 1848 aged 12, his different manifestations of capitalism began with his association with North American railways and the innovation of sleeping cars with the Pullman Company. The last years of the century saw him make his real fortune with the Carnegie Steel Company through his exploitation of the Bessemer steelmaking process. In *The Gospel of Wealth* he articulated his philanthropic views.

THE CONTEMPORARY VIEW

My childhood's desire was to get to be a man and kill a king.
Do not be fastidious; take what the gods offer.
The Man who dies thus rich, dies disgraced.

Andrew Carnegie

It was not until the advent of Bessemer that the Americans found how lavishly nature had endowed them [with high quality iron ore]. . .
The result has been to give industrial leadership to the United States.
Burton Hendrick, *The Life of Andrew Carnegie* (1932)

Being a millionaire's nice enough some wyes, but there's a wheen things money canna buy. . .

Neil Munro: *"Carnegie's Wee Lassie"*
in *Erchie, My Droll Friend (*1904)

THE WIDER VIEW

Carnegie also made his mark on Scotland. His Trusts were the means of bettering many lives through educational and public good works, most famously by his libraries as well as, more eccentrically, by hundreds of church organs. He built a much-loved summer home at Skibo Castle in Sutherland. In later years his hopes and plans for world peace were shattered by the 1914–18 War. Carnegie died in 1919.

Pity the poor millionaire, for the way of the philanthropist is hard.
Andrew Carnegie

THE COMPLETION OF THE REBUILDING OF BALMORAL CASTLE

On Queen Victoria's first visit to Scotland in 1842 she was immediately impressed by the splendours of Scottish scenery and found the people and their way of life extremely congenial. Until 1848, however, when Prince Albert leased the estate of Balmoral on upper Deeside, she had endured the smirr and rain of holidays on the west coast rather than the warmer summer climes of Aberdeenshire. Balmoral had previously belonged to Sir Robert Gordon, who had developed the deer forest and made improvements to the old castle. These improvements were continued under the personal supervision of the Prince Consort and William Smith, architect, and produced the magnificent Invergelder granite structure we see today.

Balmoral is done in the Scots Baronial style beloved of the Victorians and was to be the Queen's home for part of every year after the death of Albert in 1861. In a curious domestic sense the Royal Family's associations with Scotland and the Scottish people had become closer than at any time since 1603.

THE CONTEMPORARY VIEW

Every year my heart becomes more fixed in this dear Paradise, and so much more so now, that all had become my dear Albert's own creation, own building, own laying out. . .

Queen Victoria

THE WIDER VIEW

Victoria loved her Scottish home and developed a rapport with the lives of the country people – perhaps not best exemplified by the quaintness of John Brown – and when travelling abroad incognito she did so as Countess of Balmoral. The new links between royalty and Presbyterianism also began at this time as she regularly took communion in the Scots kirk. Her trend-setting can be seen too in the oft-photographed appearances of Victoria as highland chief, even as something of a Jacobite sympathiser.

THE "THIN RED LINE" AT BALACLAVA

The stand of the 93rd Sutherland Highlanders (later the 2nd Battalion the Argyll and Sutherland Highlanders) against Russian cavalry at the Battle of Balaclava (25 October 1854) is remembered as one of the epics of Scottish arms, not least for Sir Colin Campbell, the commander of the Highland Brigade's pre-battle injunction "There is no retreat from here, men. You must die where you stand" and the reply from the ranks "Ay, ay, Sir Colin, and needs be we'll do that".

When the line had held and the Russians turned the Highlanders were all for following up with a bayonet charge but were restrained by Sir Colin's stern cries of "93rd! 93rd! Damn all that eagerness!"

THE CONTEMPORARY VIEW

The Russians drew breath for a moment and then in one grand line charged for Balaclava. The ground flew beneath their horses' feet, gathering speed at every stride, they dashed on towards the thin red streak tipped with a line of steel.

W.H. Russell, *The Times*

THE WIDER VIEW

The "Thin Red Line" must symbolise post-Union Scottish military glory – one could equally point to the Royal Scots Greys at Waterloo; the Black Watch at Tel-el-Kebir; Piper Findlater of the Gordons, shot through both ankles, playing his comrades into action at Dargai; the relief of Lucknow, and a hundred other conflicts. The Scottish soldier lived up to Wolfe's description "a hardy and intrepid race".

An alternative view of Scotland's military record is given by the contemporary poet Hamish Henderson in his vision of a new world of peace and brotherly love "Freedom Come- all-ye"

Nae mair will the bonnie callants
Mairch tae war when oor braggarts crousely craw

Broken faimlies in lands we've herriet
Will curse Scotland the Brave nae mair, nae mair

THE TRIAL OF MADELEINE SMITH

Glasgow was shocked by the extraordinary trial of Madeleine Smith. The 22 year old daughter of a leading Glasgow architect, Madeleine was accused of poisoning her lover, Pierre Emile L'Angelier. That a young woman of good family should have a lover was bad, that he was poor and foreign was worse, that she should write uninhibited love-letters was outrageous, that she should feed him arsenic in his cocoa was infamous.

The evidence was circumstantial, though strong. Madeleine had purchased arsenic and she did have a motive to rid herself of L'Angelier (her engagement to a more suitable partner). She was defended skilfully by John Inglis, whose efforts secured a verdict of "not proven".

THE CONTEMPORARY VIEW

What a putrifying layer of debasement, lust, and hypocrisy, festering under the smooth-skinned surface of society in moral-living, church-going, theatre-hating, Sabbath-keeping Glasgow do the occurrences present out of which arose the trial of Madeline Smith!
[L'Angelier] A foreigner, with all a foreigner's lax morality, where women are concerned. . .
Had these letters of Madeline Smith's never been written, the depths of degradation to which she had sunk could never have been discovered – possibly L'Angelier would not have met his fearful death, and she, instead of the dreadful ordeal she passed, might have been the repentant wife of an honest and affectionate husband.
West of Scotland Magazine & Review, September 1857

THE WIDER VIEW

The Scots "Not Proven" verdict frequently attracts comment. Less remarked is the fact that Scotland's "third verdict" is arguably "not guilty". Until 1728, when Robert Dundas secured a return to a long-disused "not guilty" option in the trial of Carnegie of Finhaven for murdering the Earl of Strathmore, juries had traditionally to return a verdict of "proven" or "not proven" on the evidence.

THE LOCH KATRINE WATER SUPPLY SCHEME

Nineteenth century industrial cities were faced with many problems and the public health problems caused by inadequate water supplies were high on this list. Glasgow had supplemented wells with a supply from the Clyde at Dalmarnock, a scheme designed early in the century by Thomas Telford. An alternative supply from the Falls of Clyde, proposed by Henry Bell *(q.v.)*, was rejected. Other schemes were added, notably the Gorbals scheme, drawing supplies from Barrhead in Renfrewshire. By mid century the city's rapid population growth and industrial demands resulted in shortages and the prevalance of water-borne disease, such as cholera, made new, pure and copious supplies imperative.

An 1853 scheme by the private water companies to draw supplies from Loch Lubnaig failed. In 1855 Parliamentary approval was obtained for the city to buy out the private companies and draw water from Loch Katrine in the Trossachs – a distance of some 35 miles. This would supply 50 million gallons of pure water a day. The scheme was opened by Queen Victoria on 15 October 1859 and the supply became available to the city in March 1860.

THE CONTEMPORARY VIEW

Such a work is worthy of the enterprise and philanthropy of Glasgow, and I trust it will be blessed with complete success.
        Queen Victoria (speaking at the opening ceremony)

THE WIDER VIEW

The Loch Katrine scheme was part of a energetic policy of civic improvement carried through by the Glasgow City Council. "Municipal Socialism" would not have been a term that commended itself to the middle-class businessmen and industrialists who dominated the Council but their remarkable activities in public transport, slum clearance, public health, gas and electricity supply attracted international attention and Glasgow's series of International Exhibitions in 1888, 1901 and 1911 were equally noteworthy.

TOM MORRIS WINS HIS FOURTH OPEN CHAMPIONSHIP

Golf, the sport of Scottish monarchs – Queen Mary, James VI and James VII are all recorded participants – was entering a new phase in the middle years of the nineteenth century. Courses were growing both in number and sophistication, as was equipment – the "featherie" ball was giving way to the "guttie", made from gutta percha, an invention credited to a St Andrews minister, Dr. Paterson. Such improvements were transforming the skill and accuracy of play. A yet more significant transition can be detected in the appearance of the first professionals, notably "Young" Tom Morris, another native of the Home of Golf.

Morris won his first two Open Championships at Prestwick as a professional there, but it was the decision of the St Andrews club to invite him back as their first professional which set the pattern for the game's future development. He won his third Open Championship there in 1864 and his fourth in 1866.

THE CONTEMPORARY VIEW

[An amateur] *shall be a golfer who has never made for sale any golf clubs, balls, or any other articles. . . who has never carried clubs for hire after attaining the age of 15 years. . . who has never received any consideration for playing in a match or for giving lessons in the game, and who. . . has never received a money prize in an open competition.*
Rules of the first Amateur Championship, 1886

THE WIDER VIEW

This diversity of roles of the early professionals would gradually be replaced by a greater single-mindedness, even more so when Scots professionals like Willie Dunn moved across the Atlantic to the rich pickings of the emergent American game. Golf was on course to be a world sport, but only in Scotland, its cradle, was it a game for all.

THE DEATH OF
ROBERT LOUIS STEVENSON

Robert Louis Stevenson, poet, essayist and novelist, who died on December 3 1894, aged 44, at Vailima, in Samoa, was the leading Scottish writer of his age. Descended from a family of lighthouse engineers, builders of the Bell Rock *(q.v.)* and other famous lights, and on his mother's side from a race of clergy and landowners, he both rejected and celebrated his twin inheritance. Intended for the family business, he studied engineering at Edinburgh University before transferring to law. He qualified as an advocate but never practised. Troubled by ill health he spent much of his life furth of Scotland in search of a benign climate.

THE CONTEMPORARY VIEW

He had genius, sanity, gaiety, and an abiding charm of humanity which ensured him many ardent friendships.

Neil Munro

THE WIDER VIEW

Stevenson was a passionate Scot whose habit of describing himself as English was simply the manner of his age. Scotland pervades and informs his writing. His short story *The Strange Case of Dr Jekyll and Mr Hyde* exemplifies this – although ostensibly set in London, critics have pointed out that its true setting is Edinburgh and its concern with man's two natures is undeniably Scottish and Calvinist. His unfinished masterpiece *Weir of Hermiston*, set in the Pentland Hills he loved and celebrated, deals with conflict between a young idealistic dreamer and his hard-headed father, a hanging judge modelled on Lord Braxfield –"I'm a man that get's through with my day's business, and let that suffice". This theme, and Stevenson's ambivalent treatment of the Judge, reflects his own difficult relationship with his father, and indeed his country, both of whom he loved, at a distance.

Here he lies where he longed to be;
Home is the sailor, home from sea
And the hunter home from the hill.
  Robert Louis Stevenson, "Requiem"

THE FORMATION OF THE SCOTTISH TRADES UNION CONGRESS

Trade unionism in nineteenth century Scotland had been variable in effectiveness and strength. Restricted by law, unionism was best organised in mining, printing and the textile industries. In the 1870s the miners led by Alexander MacDonald had been prominent and he became, in 1874, one of the first working class Members of Parliament. Local groupings of unions in Trades Councils began to emerge in mid-century in Scotland's cities.

Scottish trades union activists became hostile to the British Trades Union Congress, viewing it as undemocratic and insufficiently representative of trades councils and the smaller unions they afforded a voice to. Employers organisations were also becoming better organised. In March 1897 the founding Scottish Trades Union Congress was held in Glasgow with some 56 organisations represented.

THE CONTEMPORARY VIEW

. . . trades unionism, co-operation and labour representation were only good so far as they led to socialism.
Keir Hardie: Speech to STUC, March 1897

. . . to see in Scotland. . . some real and practical endeavour towards an active recognition of the solidarity of the workers. . .
The Clarion (Independent Labour Party Newspaper), 1897

THE WIDER VIEW

The STUC would quickly become an important arena for left-wing politics in Scotland and play a significant part in the formation, in 1900, of the Labour Representation Committee, the forerunner of the modern Labour Party.

The STUC's power centre was its Parliamentary Committee and the first Secretary of that Committee was Margaret Irwin of the Scottish Council for Women's Trades, a noteworthy, if infrequently repeated, example of equality within the movement. Miss Irwin's role was recognised at the 1898 Congress when the President said ". . . that to Miss Irwin, more than any other man or woman in the country, was due the position of the Scottish Trade Unionists assembled there as a Congress".

THOMAS LIPTON KNIGHTED

On 10 May 1871, Thomas Johnstone Lipton, aged 21, opened a grocer's shop at 101 Stobcross Street, Glasgow. From that modest beginning grew an international food company and an enormous personal fortune. He imported butter, cheese and bacon directly from Ireland, eliminating the middle-man and selling at low prices. Lipton, the son of a poor Irish labourer turned grocer, applied the business practices of the industrial age to the organisation and marketing of his chain of shops.

His gift for publicity and imaginative development of large scale integrated enterprises facilitated by modern transport made him a millionaire by his 30th birthday. From a Glasgow based chain of shops, Liptons became an international combine with tea plantations in Ceylon and slaughter-houses in Chicago.

The passion of his later life was yacht-racing and in a vain attempt to win the *America*'s Cup he built a series of racing yachts, all named *Shamrock* in tribute to his family origins.

THE CONTEMPORARY VIEW

Direct from the tea gardens to the teapot

Lipton Advertisement

General gratification will be felt at the inclusion of Mr Lipton's name in this list [1898 Birthday Honours List]. *As a result of his own industry and capacity he has amassed very considerable wealth, which he disburses in the most generous and philanthropic fashion*

Daily Telegraph 1898

THE WIDER VIEW

Lipton, through a shared love for yacht-racing, became a close friend of King Edward VII. He was knighted, for charitable works, in 1898, appointed Knight Commander of the Royal Victorian Order (the personal gift of the sovereign) in 1901 and created a baronet in 1902. He died, unmarried, in 1931, leaving his fortune to charitable causes in Glasgow and is buried in the family lair in the city's Southern Necropolis.

THE OPENING OF
GLASGOW SCHOOL OF ART

Glasgow's history of officially sponsored art education began in 1840, but the two most significant dates in the story are 1885, when Francis H. "Fra" Newberry became head of the Glasgow School of Art, and 1899, when the new building, designed by the school's most famous alumnus Charles Rennie Mackintosh, was opened.

Newberry was a visionary teacher who did as much as any one person to bring about the flowering of the Glasgow Style. Under Newberry's direction the Glasgow School of Art achived excellence in both fine art and design. The work of Mackintosh, the Macdonald sisters, George Walton, Jessie M. King and Herbert MacNair, embracing painting, print-making, architecture, design, metal and glass work, demonstrates the wide-ranging nature of the GSA.

The city's artistic life was not, however confined to the School of Art, the "Glasgow Boys" - artists like Guthrie, Crawhall, Lavery and Henry were establishing an international reputation from the 1880s with their own brand of Impressionism.

THE CONTEMPORARY VIEW

. . . artist craftsmen have been engaged to give instruction in such subjects as Glass Staining, Pottery, Repoussé and Metal Work, Wood Carving and Book-binding, besides Artistic Needlework taught by a lady
Glasgow School of Art Annual Report, 1893

THE WIDER VIEW

The work of Glasgow School of Art graduates in the early years of the twentieth century was at the very cutting edge of modernism. Mackintosh and Margaret Macdonald for example, successfully exhibited at the 1900 Vienna Secession Exhibition. The "Glasgow Style" was widely admired and seen at other major "modernist" exhibitions in Munich, Turin, Moscow and Budapest. It embraced elements derived from Japanese art – simplicity of form and muted colours; elements derived from stylised natural forms – flowers, foliage and an admixture of Celtic imagery and design.

THE FORMATION OF THE UNITED FREE CHURCH

The bitterness within Scottish presbyterianism was evidently on the decline when the Free Church, the product of the 1843 Disruption *(q.v.)*, formed the United Free Church in 1900 with the United Presbyterian Church, created in 1847 and the heir of the Relief and Secession *(q.v.)* Churches of the eighteenth Century. The Free and the U. P. Churches shared similar views on the need for independence from the civil power and their remaining differences were largely ones of custom while the pressures making for union included widespread contemporary concerns over scientific rationalism, scepticism and social issues. Indeed even the Church of Scotland was moving towards a form of establishment less offensive to the voluntary sentiments of the Free and U.P. Churches. An Act of Union was agreed and in November 1900 celebrations of the Union took place in kirks all over Scotland. As evidence of better feeling these services were often attended by representatives of all local churches – a rapprochement inconceivable in the bitter aftermath of 1843.

THE CONTEMPORARY VIEW

One regrettable feature of this Union is that it did not embrace all sections of the Presbyterian Church in Scotland, but I believe in God's providence that will come sooner or later.
Provost Cowan speaking at St David's U. F. Church,
Kirkintilloch November 1900

THE WIDER VIEW

Provost Cowan's vision was largely fulfilled in 1929 when the U. F. Church combined with the Church of Scotland. However in 1900 not all Free Churches supported Union and a continuing Free Church – the "wee Frees" – particularly strong in the Highlands, survived. A property dispute was carried to the House of Lords where the continuing Free Church was declared legal owner of all Free Church property, an absurdity eventually reconciled by Act of Parliament.

RONALD ROSS AWARDED NOBEL PRIZE FOR MEDICINE

In 1898 Ronald Ross (1857-1932) of the Indian Medical Service demonstrated the role of the anopheles mosquito in the transmission of malaria. He later became a professor at the Liverpool School of Tropical Medicine. In 1902 his work was recognised by the Nobel Prize. He was knighted in 1911. His work was a vital step in finding methods of control or treatment of a major tropical disease.

Ross came from a Ross-shire family long-connected with India and symbolises generations of Scots who saw in the sub-continent opportunity for advancement in military or civil service and commerce.

Scots had served the Honourable East India Company even before the 1707 Union but in the later eighteenth century the movement of younger sons of the Scots middle classes and gentry to India became a flood. The influence of Henry Dundas, who controlled much of the patronage of the East India Company through his domination of the Government appointed Board of Control, in steering appointments the way of political allies was crucial.

In a sense the Scots ruled India; the list of Governors General and Viceroys includes: John Macpherson 1785-86, Gilbert Elliot 1807-13, the Marquis of Dalhousie 1847-56, the eighth Earl of Elgin 1862-63, the ninth Earl of Elgin 1894-95, the Earl of Minto 1905-10, the Marquess of Linlithgow 1936-43.

THE CONTEMPORARY VIEW

India is the corn chest for Scotland where we poor gentry must send our younger sons as we send our black cattle to the south.
Walter Scott, Letter, 1821

THE WIDER VIEW

Ross's was Scotland's first Nobel Prize. Other Scots Nobel laureates include William Ramsay (Chemistry 1904), John MacLeod (Medicine 1923), Alexander Fleming *(q.v.)* (Medicine 1945), John Boyd-Orr (Peace 1949), Alexander Todd (Chemistry 1957), and James Whyte Black (Medicine 1988).

1904

THE COMPLETION OF
THE HILL HOUSE BY
CHARLES RENNIE MACKINTOSH

When the publisher Walter Blackie was seeking an architect to design a new family home to be built in the seaside town of Helensburgh he accepted the recommendation of the designer, Talwin Morris, and engaged the young Mackintosh, one of eleven children of a Glasgow police superintendent. In so doing he gave Scotland an architectural gem which proved to have an influence on international taste and design.

Mackintosh, in his first major commission, had produced the design for the Glasgow School of Art, arguably his masterpiece, but was still comparatively unknown. The house for Blackie shows typical Mackintosh features of large cubic blocking with small windows and other vernacular characteristics like harling and a circular staircase tower, evoking Scots tower houses. The interior provides a lovely contrast, with the simple elegance of its Japanese-style motif. All of the interior was his work and demonstrates his contention that architecture is an integrated process and not simply "an envelope without contents".

THE CONTEMPORARY VIEW

Here is the house. It is not an Italian Villa, an English Mansion House, a Swiss Chalet, or a Scotch Castle. It is a dwelling House.
Mackintosh to Blackie on completion of the commission

The exotic bloom of a strange plant, not made but grown, not sensuous but chaste, not floating like a dream, but firm and decisive like the poetical vision of a fact.
Deutsche Kunst und Dekoration, 1905, on The Hill House

THE WIDER VIEW

The Mackintosh revival of recent years has brought some tat and much plagiarism as well as a belated recognition and fame which was not available to the man himself. With work like this, Scotland found an icon for the new century and a vernacular tradition invigorated and reformed.

1909

THE PUBLICATION OF
MARJORY KENNEDY FRASER'S
SONGS OF THE HEBRIDES

Daughter of a renowned singer, the arranger Marjory Kennedy-Fraser (1857-1930) has today a mixed reputation. She brought a wealth of traditional Gaelic music and song, such as "An Eriskay Love Lilt", to the attention of polite drawing-room society, but on the other hand she is accused of misunderstanding and even distorting the material which she collected. Certainly, the charge of bowdlerisation can be levelled at her methods, at her "sanitisation" of songs which gave an artless, natural expression of physical love.

Much of the music would have been lost to the wider world had it not been for her work and her abilities as arranger and presenter. A song like "Kismul's Galley" conveys much of the bravado of the MacNeils of Barra, a chief of which clan declined a place on Noah's Ark because he already had a fine vessel of his own.

THE CONTEMPORARY VIEW

In a little over twenty-four hours, I had sailed, I felt, out of the twentieth century back at least to the 1600s.

> Marjory Kennedy-Fraser writing about the beginnings of her collecting on Eriskay

Bheir mi o ro bhan o
Bheir mi or ro bhan i;
Bheir mi or ro o ho,
Sad am I without thee
Thou'rt the music of my heart,
Harp of joy, oh! chruit mo chridhe
Moon of guidance by night,
Strength and light thou'rt to me.

> "An Eriskay Love Lilt"

THE WIDER VIEW

Scholar she may not have been, but Kennedy-Fraser has proved irreplaceable. In concert-hall and recording studio the songs live on, songs which might have been lost in the social and cultural changes which overtook the Islands in this century.

THE FIRST WORLD WAR

The history of the Great War in Scotland is one of enthusiasm of all kinds. Harry McShane, the Glasgow socialist activist, told of an early enthusiasm – "Men rushed to join the army hoping the war wouldn't be all over by the time they got to the front". The press and the churches united to present the war as a just and holy cause, and the volunteers who enlisted in proportionately greater numbers than other parts of Britain were enthusiastic fighters – the "ladies from Hell" – as the enemy were supposed to have called the kilted regiments.

On the home front, too, the workers were uninhibited in production while they could also advance their socialist beliefs through industrial action like the "tuppence an hour" strike in 1915. In the same year the housewives of Glasgow led a rent strike, arguing that total war did not justify profiteering by landlords.

THE CONTEMPORARY VIEW

And Chae swore that he still believed the War would bring a good thing to the world, it would end the armies and the fighting forever, the day of socialism at last would dawn, the common folk had seen what their guns could do and right soon they'd use them when once they came back.

Lewis Grassic Gibbon, *Sunset Song*

While my father is a prisoner in Germany, the landlord is attacking our home.

Rent strike placard

THE WIDER VIEW

The casualties of war have been estimated at approaching one tenth of the adult male population; surprisingly, disillusionment was not universal, but the political education of the working class was completed. They had, after all, fought a capitalist war, they had closed ranks for the duration, but in future their votes would be reserved for their own ends.

1919

THE "40 HOURS" STRIKE AND GEORGE SQUARE DEMONSTRATION

The red flag of Bolshevism flew in Glasgow's George Square, heads were broken in the rioting, labour leaders like Willie Gallacher and Mannie Shinwell were arrested, tanks stood in readiness in the Meat Market in Duke Street. The demonstration on 31 January backed a move for a 40 hour working week, intended to ease the mounting unemployment which had followed the post-War economic boom.

The Liberal Coalition Government, just two years after the Russian Revolution, was alarmed at the possibilities of revolution and conscious of a deep-rooted tradition of left-wing politics on "Red" Clydeside. In fact the post-war election had returned few Labour M.P.s and fewer Bolshevik sympathisers. There was a broad church of left activists, prone to internal dissension – Gallacher argued for a 30 hour week campaign – but the labour and trade union movement had settled on the 40 hour slogan and had filled George Square. Strikes throughout Scotland had preceded the demonstration and the alarmed authorities overreacted and brought in troops and large numbers of special constables.

THE CONTEMPORARY VIEW

I fail to see how, whether morally justified or nor, a popular revolt in present circumstances could be successful in Britain where political power is held by the capitalist. . . a bloody revolution is far too slow, whether viewed from the standpoint of democracy or expediency. I prefer the I.L.P. (Independent Labour Party) *policy of relying more upon brains than bullets.*

John Wheatley, in an article rejecting
revolutionary and syndicalist tactics

THE WIDER VIEW

The "Forty Hours" Strike was called off in early February but militancy was a permanent feature of the inter-war Scottish political scene. George Square was perhaps the closest the country came to a revolutionary moment with industrial rather than political action remaining the preferred route.

RAMSAY MACDONALD BECOMES PRIME MINISTER

Born in Lossiemouth, James Ramsay MacDonald's pacifist views during the Great War gave him a reputation as a left-winger within the Labour party, a reputation which would be severely tested in years to come. His oratory and appearance, however, appealed to the British public and helped to make Labour electorally respectable. Stanley Baldwin having resigned over the free trade issue, and despite the Conservatives remaining the largest party, Labour was able to form its first-ever administration in January 1924. John Wheatley, one of the "Red Clydesiders", the Glasgow I.L.P. group, was appointed Health Minister and introduced a Housing Act, which encouraged slum clearance and municipal housebuilding. This was the Government's only significant measure of social reform and its inaction was deeply disappointing to much of MacDonald's party. However it was foreign policy and the "Red Scare" over the Zinoviev Letter which forced an election. Once more the association in people's minds between socialism and Bolshevism helped bring Baldwin back to power in November 1924.

THE CONTEMPORARY VIEW

[He] *did not think that the Labour Government would take office as a minority government to do little things in administration which they could do little better than the Liberals or the Tories. They were returned to Parliament to make fundamental changes.*

James Maxton

THE WIDER VIEW

There was an inevitable sense of anti-climax at the meagre results of MacDonald's short-lived ministry and the times were not auspicious either when he formed his second administration in 1929, just as the Wall Street crash signalled the onset of the Great Depression. Disillusionment among Labour supporters was not complete, however, until 1931 when to their derision MacDonald appeared at the head of a "National" Government, composed almost entirely of Conservatives.

THE PUBLICATION OF "A DRUNK MAN LOOKS AT THE THISTLE"

The inter-war years saw a flowering of Scottish literature, often termed "The Scottish Renaissance" and contemporary poets entitled themselves the "New Makars" – in conscious reference to the golden age of Dunbar and Douglas (q.v.).

The dominant figure was Christopher Grieve (1892-1978), writing under the pen-name of Hugh MacDiarmid. MacDiarmid's work was notable for its use of a determinedly non-demotic Scots, which like his life and opinions, exemplified the line from his greatest work "A Drunk Man Looks at the Thistle":

I'll hae nae hauf-way hoose, but aye be whaur
Extremes meet

Novelists of quality emerged in the period. James Leslie Mitchell (1901-1935), writing as Lewis Grassic Gibbon, reflected the speech of his native North-East in his masterly trilogy *A Scots Quair*, published between 1932 and 1936. An imagination rooted in the land and the experiences of the people of his native Highlands characterised the novels of Neil Gunn (1891- 1973), particularly in his masterpiece, *The Silver Darlings*, published in 1942. This tells of a boy's coming to maturity and his rites of passage in the search for herring – the "silver darlings" of the title.

While Gunn, MacDiarmid and Gibbon dominate the period, their pre-eminence should not obscure the achievement of many contemporaries, such as the much under-rated novelist Eric Linklater (1889-1974), Naomi Mitchison (1897-) and the poet William Soutar (1898- 1943).

THE CONTEMPORARY VIEW

A Scottish poet maun assume
The burden o' his people's doom
And dee to brak' their livin' tomb
   MacDiarmid, *A Drunk Man Looks at the Thistle*

THE WIDER VIEW

The Scottish Renaissance was characterised by rejection of a debased and sentimentalised use of Scots and by political commitment. As the above extract suggests, it also stressed the centrality of the writer's role in the re-making of the nation.

ALEXANDER FLEMING
DISCOVERS PENICILLIN

Alexander Fleming (1881-1955), an Ayrshire farmer's son, went to London at 14 and worked as a shipping clerk for five years before entering medical school. After qualifying he made a career in bacteriology, pioneering new treatments for typhoid and syphilis. After war service in the Medical Corps he returned to research at St Mary's Hospital, London, where, in 1928 he noticed the effect of an accidental growth of *penicillium notatum* mould on a staphylococcus culture. Experiment proved that the active ingredient, which he christened penicillin, had an antibiotic action effective against a wide range of organisms.

The Second World War proved a spur to the practical exploitation of penicillin and Howard Florey and Ernst Chain developed a production method and United States laboratories manufactured penicillin in quantity, initially for military use. By the end of the war supplies were coming into civilian use. Fleming was knighted in 1944 and he, Florey and Chain shared the 1945 Nobel Prize for Medicine.

THE CONTEMPORARY VIEW

. . . the world will acclaim a medical advance "great" in proportion to the curative effects it brings, and on this count alone Sir Alexander Fleming has his place among the immortals.

British Medical Journal, 1955

All the same, the spores didn't just stand up. . . and say "I produce an antibiotic, you know."

Sir Alexander Fleming

THE WIDER VIEW

Fleming demonstrates what Pasteur described as the prepared mind. Years searching for the "magic bullet", a safe but powerful antibiotic, meant that when he saw the pencillium mould attacking the staphylococcus culture he knew its significance. Practical use was long delayed and Florey and Chain deservedly shared the credit. However Fleming it was who became an international folk hero, had his biography written by André Maurois and is buried in St Paul's Cathedral.

1929

THE FIRST TELEVISION
SERVICE STARTS

In September 1929 the world's first television service started transmission from the BBC's London radio transmitter. Programmes went out after midnight when the radio service closed down. The mechanically scanned television system used was first publicly demonstrated in 1925 by its inventor John Logie Baird. Baird, a son of the manse, was born in Helensburgh, Dumbartonshire in 1888. He trained in electrical engineering at the Royal Technical College, Glasgow, and from an early age showed an interest in photography and telecommunications.

By 1929 he had also successfully demonstrated three dimensional colour televsion, transmitted television pictures across the Atlantic, invented fibre optics and produced an infra-red night viewing system. He continued to work on television and related fields and was involved in wartime defence projects while privately developing an electronic system of high definition, three dimensional colour television. He died in 1946, having gained little financial reward from his work.

Baird was obliged to work through the BBC, which was initially unenthusiastic about television. His difficult relationship with its auto-cratic Director General, John Reith, a Glasgow college contemporary, did little to advance his cause. After competitive trials the BBC adopted the rival Marconi-EMI electronic system in 1936.

THE CONTEMPORARY VIEW

*What a marvellous discovery you have made. . . You have put
something in my room which will never let me forget how strange is
this world – and how unknown.*
Prime Minister J. Ramsay MacDonald to John Logie Baird

A social menace of the first magnitude
Sir John Reith on television

THE WIDER VIEW

The long search for television involved researchers and inventors in all parts of the world. Baird's lack of commercial success should not disguise his technological innovation and clear priority in demonstrating a practical system of televsion.

THE LAUNCH OF RMS *QUEEN MARY*

This, the best known and most affectionately remembered of the great ocean liners was launched at John Brown's shipyard, Clydebank in September 1934. The *Mary* was designed to epitomise luxury and yet was also a symbol of hope for the people of Clydebank when work restarted on No. 534 after a long suspension during the Depression. Massive in scale at 1,019 feet in length and displacing 81,237 tons, her 12 decks could accommodate over 2,000 passengers in three classes. Her interior design was of restrained Art Deco.

During World War Two *Queen Mary* was fitted out in Sydney as a troopship and after the United States' entry into the War was used to ferry a whole division at a time across to the UK. Her high speed gave her a measure of invulnerability to U-boat attack. She and her sister ship *Queen Elizabeth* (launched in September 1938) together moved some one and half million troops.

The *Mary* was refitted for luxury travel after the war but the advent of jet aircraft meant the end for the Atlantic liner. Eventually she was losing $1.8 million a year and in September 1967 sailed from New York for the last time.

THE CONTEMPORARY VIEW

New York to Gourock 16,683 souls aboard. New York 25 July 1943. Gourock 30 July 1943. 3,353 miles, 4 days, 20 hours, 42 minutes. 28.73 knots. The greatest number of human beings ever embarked on one vessel.

Log of RMS *Queen Mary*

THE WIDER VIEW

Queen Mary lingers on as a floating maritime museum and convention centre in Long Beach, California. Almost as lost as the Atlantic liner has been the proud tradition of shipbuilding on the Clyde, now reduced to three yards on the whole river.

1935

JOHN BUCHAN BECOMES LORD TWEEDSMUIR, GOVERNOR GENERAL OF CANADA

Born in 1875 in Perth, the son of a Free Church minister, Buchan was a brilliant scholar who, like Disraeli, combined literary success with a career in public life. After studying at Glasgow and Oxford Universities he went to South Africa as one of " Milner's young men" to assist in post-Boer War reconstruction. While there he garnered material for his African books such as *Prester John* and characters like Peter Pienaar and Richard Hannay – a strongly developed sense of place being characteristic of much of his work. Buchan is best remembered for what he called his "shockers" – sensational adventure novels, crammed full of action, often with hunted fugitives in crosscountry chases, as in *The Thirty-Nine Steps*, with its echoes of Stevenson. These have remained popular, despite some dated attitudes and suspect values, largely because of their intense readability. The historical novels, like *Midwinter*, his historical biographies of Scott and Montrose, and to many, his most appealing character Dickson McCunn, the retired Glasgow grocer of *Huntingtower*, reflect his varied talents.

THE CONTEMPORARY VIEW

When we were little, wandering boys,
And every hill was blue and high,
On ballad ways and martial joys
We fed our fancies, you and I.
With Bruce we crouched in bracken shade,
With Douglas charged the Paynim foes;
And oft in moorland noons I played
Colkitto to your grave Montrose.
　　Buchan's dedication in *Montrose*

THE WIDER VIEW

At the end of his life, Buchan places the semi-autobiographical figure of the dying lawyer-politician Sir Edward Leithen in the vast Canadian landscape of the last, darkest and greatest of his novels *Sick Heart River*. In this work, as in all his writing, the concept of duty and responsibility, both to others and to one's own soul, is a dominant element.

THE FOUNDATION OF THE IONA COMMUNITY

1938, Iona and the Govan shipyards form an unlikely seed-bed for the closest approach to a religious order seen in Scottish presbyterianism. The link is found in the charismatic, contradictory and controversial figure of George MacLeod. He won the Military Cross during the First World War, later becoming a pacifist and nuclear disarmer. A socialist, he inherited a baronetcy but never used the title. In 1967 he accepted a life peerage, becoming Lord MacLeod of Fiunary. A product of the Kirk establishment, he was often at odds with it but became Moderator in 1957 and saw his unilateralist views become accepted in the General Assembly in 1986.

In the 1930s, as Minister at Govan Old Parish Church, he saw the human waste caused by unemployment. Equally concerned about the health of the Kirk and its response to the problems of the day, he resolved to restore the ruins of St Columba's *(q.v.)* Abbey of Iona, utilising the skills of unemployed tradesmen and young ministers, banded together as a community and rediscovering the Columban ideals of mission, community and service.

THE CONTEMPORARY VIEW

In Iona of my heart, Iona of my love,
Instead of monk's voices shall be lowing of cattle;
But ere the world come to an end,
Iona shall be as it was.

St Columba (521–597)

It would be the modern counterpart of St Columba's original intention: the New Light of Protestantism would be lit to meet our day, as his Lamp met his.

George MacLeod (1895–1991)

THE WIDER VIEW

The Abbey was restored and an ecumenical centre established which attracts visitors from all round the world. The Community, true to MacLeod's vision, did not confine itself to the work on the island but carried its message to urban Scotland.

THE SECOND WORLD WAR

The coming of war in September 1939 involved Scottish civilians in an unprecedented way. The destruction of towns like Guernica during the Spanish Civil War had convinced everyone that "the bomber will always get through" and bomb and gas attacks on civilian centres were anticipated and prepared for. Gas masks were issued, bomb shelters constructed, evacuation of women and children from major target cities organised, the registration and organisation of the population was undertaken on a remarkable scale.

Scotland's first encounter with war was the torpedoing, on 3 September, of the transatlantic liner *Athenia* outward bound from the Clyde. Scotland experienced the war's first air raid on 16th October, when bombers attacked Rosyth naval base, inflicting minor damage and losing three aircraft in the process. Two days earlier a U-boat had sunk the battleship *Royal Oak* with the loss of 833 crew.

THE CONTEMPORARY VIEW

Steel struts for the reinforcement of tenement closes to turn them into air-raid shelters will arrive in Glasgow this morning. Material sufficient for 20,000 tenements is to be provided.
Scottish Daily Express, 1 September 1939

The present war will make service demands on women folk to a far greater extent than any previous war has ever done, and the call for volunteers. . . will not. . . go unheeded by the women of Tweeddale.
Peeblesshire & South Midlothian Advertiser, 22 September 1939

THE WIDER VIEW

The Peeblesshire editor was right. Women's involvement in war, whether in the armed services, in munitions, on the land, as blitz victims and sufferers of rationing, was to be total. While the war did not produce specific legislative change, in the way that the 1914–18 war had brought about votes for women, nonetheless its effects on women's place in society was profound.

THE FORMATION OF THE NORTH OF SCOTLAND HYDRO-ELECTRIC BOARD

The idea of using Scotland's copious water power to generate electricity was well established, Greenock had an experimental plant installed in 1885. Various Highland shooting lodges were electrified and in 1896 the British Aluminimum Company supplied their Kinlochleven works from the Falls of Foyers scheme. Public hydroelectric supply started in the 1920s and 30s with schemes in the Loch Ericht and Loch Rannoch areas.

During the Second World War, Thomas Johnston, the Secretary of State for Scotland, established a Committee of Enquiry into hydro-electricity. The report, published in December 1942, argued for the establishment of a public corporation to run large scale power generation and to promote the regeneration of the Highlands. Johnston, backed by his all-party Council of State of ex-Secretaries of State, secured government support for the scheme and steered the legislation through Parliament. The new Board was established by September 1943, its first project being the Loch Sloy scheme on Loch Lomondside.

THE CONTEMPORARY VIEW

. . . the Hydro Board. . . which is by statute not only a generator of electricity, but is a distributor of it over 74% of the land area of Scotland; and which is more than that: it is a Board enjoined to promote and encourage the economic and social welfare of the Highlands.

Tom Johnston, *Memories*

THE WIDER VIEW

Johnston, from his earliest days in Kirkintilloch, had been an advocate of community and collective action. The Hydro Board, with its wide social remit, was very much his creation and Johnston became an energetic and visionary Chairman of the Board from 1946 until 1959 by when the installed capacity of their schemes had risen to over one million kilowatts.

The formation of the Highlands and Islands Development Board in 1965 continued the pattern of Government involvement in the area's economic development.

THE FIRST EDINBURGH FESTIVAL

The idea for a post-war festival of music and drama emerged in discussions in 1944 between Rudolf Bing of the Glyndbourne Opera House and Harvey Wood, the Scottish representative of the British Council. With Continental Europe in ruins, the great international festivals would be slow to re-establish themselves and Bing saw an opportunity for a British-based Festival. Wood and Bing put the idea to the Edinburgh City Council and gained their enthusiasm and financial support.

The first festival, with Bing as Director, established the standard for the years to come – international performers of the highest quality performed in Edinburgh, perhaps most memorable being the appearance of the Vienna Philharmonic with their pre-war conductor Bruno Walter – although comment was made about the comparative absence of Scottish performers and works.

This criticism was unforgettably answered in 1948 by the Tyrone Guthrie production, the first for 396 years, of David Lyndsay's *Thrie Estaitis (q.v.)*, staged in the Church of Scotland's Assembly Hall – a far cry from the days when the Kirk condemned the theatre.

THE CONTEMPORARY VIEW

We wish to provide the world with a centre where, year after year, all that is best in Music, Drama and the Visual Arts can be seen and heard in ideal surroundings.

Lord Provost Sir John Falconer in 1947
Festival Souvenir Programme

THE WIDER VIEW

The time was ripe in 1947 for launching an enterprise like the Edinburgh Festival – during the war state involvement in the Arts had developed under C.E.M.A. (the Council for Encouragement of Music and the Arts), which in 1946 became the Arts Council. The need of the citizen for culture had taken its proper place among the other, more material needs, which the new welfare state would address.

THE SIGNING OF THE NATIONAL COVENANT

In the immediate post-war years, with a Labour Government of notably centralising tendency, the nationalist political tradition was at a low ebb – at least as far as representation at Westminster was concerned. "King" John MacCormick had been the torch-bearer of this tradition, although he had failed to win over people to his view of limited devolution, or Home Rule, and in 1942 he left the Scottish National Party. He had failed in elections, standing as a Liberal and later as a "National" candidate.

By 1949 his and other Home Rule advocates' best hope seemed to lie in the Scottish Convention, which rapidly organised a new Scottish National Covenant (a conscious echo of the Covenant of 1638 *(q.v.)* although this time without religious clauses), a great petition which called for devolution of political power within the United Kingdom. It gathered two million signatures and was presented to Parliament with great hopes.

THE CONTEMPORARY VIEW

We, the people of Scotland who subscribe this Engagement, declare our belief that reform in the constitution of our country is necessary to secure good government in accordance with our Scottish traditions. . .

. . . we pledge ourselves, in all loyalty to the Crown and within the framework of the United Kingdom to do everything in our power to secure for Scotland a Parliament with adequate legislative authority in Scottish affairs

The National Covenant, 1949

THE WIDER VIEW

The Covenant was more or less totally ignored. The Government was growing tired and constitutional changes were risky in uncertain economic times, the Scottish Secretary Arthur Woodburn was a fervent anti-devolutionist. On the other hand, the experience of mass action, publicity and mass education proved invaluable at a time when the SNP, under Dr Robert MacIntyre, was undergoing a root and branch reorganisation.

THE DEATH OF SIR HARRY LAUDER

Harry Lauder, who died on 26 February 1950, was for most of the world the archetypal Scotsman. His stage image of kilt and curly walking stick, his mixture of comic songs, his interspersed patter, often on the theme of his meanness and his effective use of more serious songs such as "The End of the Road", created or fortified a powerful, if unrealistic, Scottish image.

Born in Portobello in 1870 and brought up in Arbroath, where he first performed on stage, he worked as a miner before going into the theatre. An early success on the London music-hall stage, Lauder exported his brand of Scottishness to the United States, where he toured annually from 1907, and to the Commonwealth. His main appeal was to the Scottish diaspora but his consummate stage skills and fine voice earned him wide popularity.

Lauder was an active recruiter and troop entertainer during the First World War, a war in which his only son John, a Captain in the Argyll and Sutherland Highlanders, was killed. He was knighted for this work in 1919 – perhaps the first performer from music hall, as opposed to legitimate theatre, to be so honoured.

THE CONTEMPORARY VIEW

First a mill boy, then a miner, now is what the people have made him.
Lauder on Lauder, from *Who's Who*

Lauder, like Barrie, had the rare ability to lay his finger in that spot in the human heart where tears and laughter are interchangeable.
Glasgow Herald, Leader Column, 27 February 1950

THE WIDER VIEW

Lauder was in a long tradition of "Scotch comics". He was, however, more than that. For good or ill he did much to shape Scotland's international image. He was also one of the greatest musical entertainers in the heyday of music-hall.

THE U.C.S. WORK-IN

By 1971 Neil Munro's famous "ship-shop" of the upper Clyde had been reduced to five shipyards. These were linked in a consortium named Upper Clyde Shipbuilders and under the Conservative Government of Edward Heath there had been a series of moves towards rationalisation, selling off and liquidation of parts of the consortium – proposals from the so-called "Three Wise Men". Against this there arose a novel form of organised and peaceful resistance by a work force.

The unions in the yard formed a Joint Shop Stewards Co-Ordinating Committee which came up with the idea of a "work-in", using 300 of the men as the visible manifestation of a determination to carry on working as normal. Public support throughout Scotland was immense and eventually, in February 1972, the Heath Government conceded the continuing existence of three yards under the banner of Govan Shipbuilders and inducements for an American buyer – Marathon – for Clydebank.

THE CONTEMPORARY VIEW

No title, no rank, no establishment honour can compare with the privilege of belonging to the Scottish working class. That is what I want to say on behalf of UCS workers. . . Government action has projected us into the front rank of the battle against the policies of redundancies and closures. They picked the wrong people!

Jimmy Reid

THE WIDER VIEW

There were charismatic figures like Reid among the stewards and for a time work-ins looked like replacing strikes or sit-ins, as ways of demonstrating that workers were really fighting for the right to work. In the longer term, sadly, the haemorrhage continued of Scotland's industrial base – of Linwood, of Gartcosh, of Ravenscraig, of the pits – –and the shipyards themselves are only hanging on by the slenderest thread.

THE FIRST OIL FROM THE NORTH SEA

Gas had been produced from the North Sea during the 1960s but the first oil major oil find was in the Forties field in 1970, swiftly followed by the Brent field. The first oil from the Forties field, 180 kilometres east of Aberdeen, was landed by pipeline at Cruden Bay, near Peterhead, in November 1975 although oil from the Argyll field had been previously landed by tanker in June 1975.

The exploration phase gave some work to the declining Scottish shipbuilding industry but the exploitation of the North Sea fields required novel rigs and production platforms, mostly constructed in bleak and unsightly purpose built facilities which later began to close in the same way as had the traditional shipyards. By the early 1980s North Sea oil and gas represented 4% of Britain's Gross Domestic Product and a major industrial infrastructure had been developed to meet the needs of the off-shore industry.

THE CONTEMPORARY VIEW

Oil Industry Employment at 30 April 1975

Inverness & Easter Ross	5195
Remainder of Highlands & Islands	2350
North East	7635
Tayside	755
East Central	1970
West Central	1010
	18915

Department of Employment

THE WIDER VIEW

"It's Scotland's Oil" was one of the great political slogans of the Seventies, but in the end it failed to sweep the Scottish National Party to power and the financial reservoir that was the North Sea went to bolster a failing British economy and subsidise a generation of benefit payments. Aberdeen and Shetland echoed to the clatter of countless helicopters, but beyond a few areas the impact on technological advance was disappointing, while the Piper Alpha disaster of 1988 showed another face altogether. Perhaps the new frontier, west of Shetland, opened up in 1994 will tell a different story.

THE REFERENDUM ON THE SCOTLAND AND WALES ACT

After the popular sentiment of the National Covenant *(q.v.)* in 1949 the Home Rule movement was at a low ebb in the 1950s and 60s. A revival was signalled by Winifred Ewing's by-election victory for the Scottish National Party at Hamilton in 1967. James Callaghan's Labour Government introduced a measure to give a degree of home rule to Scotland and Wales, subject to public approval in a referendum.

In an amendment to the Act, the Scots-born Labour MP for Islington, George Cunningham, ensured the inclusion of a requirement for 40% of the total electoral register to vote "yes" before it would held to have been approved. This effectively made abstainers "no" voters.

Cunningham's ingenious constitutional novelty worked. There was a narrow majority at the referendum held on 1st March in favour of devolution, but as only 33% of the electorate voted for devolution the 40% barrier was not reached and the Act lapsed.

THE CONTEMPORARY VIEW

> *. . . if the present opportunity is missed I cannot see Parliament picking up this issue again for many years.*
>
> James Callaghan M.P., Prime Minister,
> speaking in Glasgow, February 1979

> *. . . the Assembly. . . will weaken Scotland's voice in Westminster and the Government.*
>
> Teddy Taylor, MP, Shadow Secretary of State,
> speaking at an anti-devolution rally, February 1979

THE WIDER VIEW

Scotland's lack of enthusiasm for devolution, particularly marked in rural areas, was evident. The Act was promoted, with less than total commitment, by a failing and unpopular Government. Support for and opposition to devolution transcended party differences with Yes and No campaigns creating strange alliances. Lord Home, the former Conservative Prime Minister, campaigned for a "no" vote in order to clear the way for a better devolution measure. Margaret Thatcher's Conservative administration, elected in May 1979, showed no interest in the subject.

1988

MARGARET THATCHER'S "SERMON ON THE MOUND"

Despite the Union of Parliaments, which, as Mrs Howden in Scott's *Heart of Midlothian* remarked, meant ". . . when we had a king, and a chancellor and parliament men o' our ain, we could aye peeble them wi' stanes when they werena gude bairns – But naebody's nails can reach the length o' Lunnon", an autonomous political life continued. One focus for this was the General Assembly of the Church of Scotland. During the Premiership of Margaret Thatcher (1979-1990), the Assembly regularly clashed with the Government on a wide range of social, economic and international issues.

The Prime Minister's visit to the opening session of the 1988 Assembly was not unusual – what was unusual was her wish to be invited to address the Assembly. This provoked division, some on the political left objected to the proposal, most felt that courtesy and propriety demanded a hearing for the Queen's first minister at the national church's General Assembly

THE CONTEMPORARY VIEW

It is on the family that we in Government build our own policies for welfare, education and care. . .

. . . intervention by the state must never become so great that it effectively removes personal responsibility. . .

Margaret Thatcher, 21 May 1988

a very selective and distorted view of the Gospel. . . lacking in a sense of community.

Rev. Paraic Reamon, on Mrs Thatcher's speech

THE WIDER VIEW

The speech was anti-climactic, being more of a personal spiritual than a political manifesto. Its perceived individualism and neglect of a wider community than the family emphasised one of the defining distinctions between much Scottish thought and the doctrines of Thatcherite conservatism.

Afterwards, in a widely applauded gesture, the Moderator, Professor James Whyte, courteously presented Mrs Thatcher with two Kirk reports, both highly critical of her Government, on housing and the distribution of income.

KINGS AND QUEENS OF SCOTS
FROM KENNETH MACALPIN

Monarch	Born	Reign from	Reign to	Notes
Kenneth I	?	843	858	First King of Alba – the united kingdom of Picts and Scots.
Donald I	?	858	862	Brother of Kenneth I.
Constantine I	?	863	877	Son of Kenneth I. Killed in battle.
Aed	?	877	878	Son of Kenneth I.
Giric	?	878	889	Son of Donald I. Deposed.
Eochaid	?	878	889	Grandson of Kenneth I in female line.
Donald II	?	889	900	Son of Constantine I. Killed.
Constantine II	?	900	943	Son of Aed. Abdicated & entered monastery. Died c.952
Malcolm I	?	943	954	Son of Donald II. Killed in battle.
Indulf	?	954	962	Son of Constantine II. Added Edinburgh to Kingdom of Alba.
Dubh	?	962	967	Son of Malcolm I.
Culen	?	967	971	Son of Indulf.
Kenneth II	?	971	995	Brother of Dubh. Murdered.
Constantine III	?	995	997	Son of Culen. Killed by Kenneth III.
Kenneth III	?	997	1005	Son of Dubh. Killed by Malcolm II.
Malcolm II	c.954	1005	1034	Son of Kenneth II. Added Lothian and Strathclyde to Alba.
Duncan I	c.1010	1034	1040	Grandson of Malcolm II in female line. Killed by Macbeth.
Macbeth	c.1005	1040	1057	Grandson of Malcolm II. Killed by Malcolm III.
Lulach	c.1032	1057	1058	Stepson of Macbeth. Killed by Malcolm III.
Malcolm III	c.1031	1058	1093	"Canmore". Son of Duncan I. Died in battle.
Donald III	c.1033	1093	1094	"Donald Bane". Son of Duncan I. Deposed by Duncan II.

Monarch	Born	Reign from	Reign to	Notes
Duncan II	c.1060	1094	1094	Son of Malcolm III. Killed by Donald III.
Donald III(Restored)		1094	1097	Deposed by Edgar. Died c.1100.
Edgar	c.1074	1097	1107	Son of Malcolm III.
Alexander I	c.1077	1107	1124	Son of Malcolm III. No legitimate heirs.
David I	c.1085	1124	1153	Son of Malcolm III.
Malcolm IV	c.1141	1153	1165	"The Maiden". Grandson of David I. Died unmarried.
William I	c.1142	1165	1214	"William the Lion". Grandson of David I.
Alexander II	1198	1214	1249	Son of William I.
Alexander III	1241	1249	1286	Son of Alexander II. Killed in accident.
Margaret	1283	1286	1290	"Maid of Norway". Granddaughter of Alexander III. Died while travelling to Scotland.
Interregnum	Competition for Crown.			Adjudicated by Edward I of England.
John	c.1250	1292	1296	Great-great-great-grandson of David I. Deposed 1296.
Interregnum	Edward I governs Scotland directly.			
Robert I	1274	1306	1329	"The Bruce". Seizes throne. Great-great-great-great-grandson of David I
David II	1324	1329	1371	Son of Robert I. Died without heir.
Robert II	1316	1371	1390	House of Stewart. Grandson of Robert I in female line.
Robert III	c.1337	1390	1406	Baptismal name John. Crowned as Robert III. Son of Robert II.
James I	1394	1406	1437	Son of Robert III. Murdered by Atholl conspiracy.
James II	1430	1437	1460	Son of James I. Killed by exploding cannon.
James III	1452	1460	1488	Son of James II. Killed at Battle of Sauchieburn.
James IV	1473	1488	1513	Son of James III. Killed at Battle of Flodden.
James V	1512	1513	1542	Son of James IV.

Monarch	Born	Reign from	Reign to	Notes
Mary	1542	1542	1567	Daughter of James V. Abdicated 1567. Executed by Elizabeth of England 1587.
James VI	1566	1567	1625	Son of Mary by marriage to Darnley. Succeeded to English throne 1603 through descent from Henry VII
Charles I	1600	1625	1649	Son of James VI. Executed.
Charles II	1630	1649	1685	Son of Charles I. Crowned at Scone 1651. In exile 1651–1660.
James VII	1633	1685	1689	Son of Charles II. Deposed by Convention of Estates, 4 April 1689.
William II and	1650	1689	1702	Grandson of Charles I.
Mary II	1662	1689	1694	Daughter of James VII.
Anne	1665	1702	1707	Daughter of James VII. On 1st April 1707 the Union of Parliaments extinguished the Kingdoms of Scotland and England replacing them with the new United Kingdom of Great Britain. Queen Anne died in 1714 and was succeeded by George I of the House of Hanover – the great grandson of James VI by the female line.

Notes

1   The dates prior to the eleventh century are uncertain and sources are confused and often contradictory.
2   The seventeenth century entries reflect Scottish practice and designations.
3   The Old Pretender (James VIII *de jure*) was the son of James VII and the elder brother of Queen Anne. Charles Edward Stewart "The Young Pretender" was the elder son of the above. He died in 1788 without heirs. The last of the male Stewart line was Charles Edward's younger brother, Henry, Cardinal York, who died in 1805.

SCOTLAND'S CAPITAL

The idea of a capital city, the permanent seat of government, administration, law and the residence of a head of state, is comparatively modern. In Scotland, until the fifteenth century, it would have been difficult to identify any town as the capital. In earlier centuries the administration of the country was in the hands of a small number of Royal officials, often clerics – in default of a literate laity – who accompanied the sovereign on his travels. Charters and other official documents are dated from wherever the Court was in residence. A number of towns became favoured as Royal residences, for strategic as well as for personal reasons. Roxburgh Castle in the Borders was an early favoured Royal residence and was the birthplace of Alexander III. Robert the Bruce built a country home at Mains of Cardross, near Dumbarton, and was to die there in 1329. Among other places where the Court resided – Dunfermline, Edinburgh, Falkland, Forteviot, Linlithgow, Perth, St Andrews, Scone and Stirling – all regularly performed one or other of the roles of a capital at different times.

DUNFERMLINE

The King sits in Dunfermling toune,
Drinking the blude-red wine:

So starts the famous ballad of "Sir Patrick Spens" and many Scottish Kings sat in Dunfermline. The Abbey of Dunfermline was founded by St Margaret, the wife of Malcolm Canmore, but Dunfermline was already by that time an established as a favoured Royal residence. The memory and tradition of the Royal Saint attracted other monarchs to the town and the Abbey. The body of Robert the Bruce is just one of many Royal interments in the Abbey. The last Scottish-born King, Charles I, was born in Dunfermline in 1600.

EDINBURGH

The modern capital of Scotland was not incorporated into the Kingdom of Alba until about a hundred years after the foundation of the Kingdom by Kenneth MacAlpin. The residences of the Castle and the guest quarters of King David I's foundation of Holyrood Abbey provided a base for the Court but the modern institutions of government first started to settle in Edinburgh with the creation of a permanently based law court in the Court of Session in 1532. Parliament Hall, Scotland's first purpose built seat for its legislature, was erected in 1639. James III was the first king to regularly stay in Edinburgh, which had one obvious drawback for a capital city – it lay on the well-trodden invasion route from England. St Margaret founded the chapel on the summit of the castle rock, the oldest surviving example of Norman architecture in Scotland. Less sacred associations of the castle include the murder of the 6th Earl of Douglas and his young brother by the Governor, Sir William Crichton, at the "Black Dinner" in 1440:

> *Edinburgh castle, towne and tower,*
> *God grant ye sink for sin!*
> *And that for the black denner*
> *Yerl Douglas gat therein.*

While the Castle on its rock was defensible, the more comfortable residence of Holyrood was not. Holyrood began its transformation from Abbey into a Royal Palace under James IV although the present building is essentially the reconstruction of the 1670s under Charles II.

FALKLAND
Under the Stewarts Falkland became a favoured hunting seat, with the old castle of the Earls of Fife being used until the time of James IV when the construction of Falkland Palace was commenced. Falkland could never be considered as the capital of Scotland except in the sense that where the Royal court was, there, for the time being, was also the seat of administration.

FORTEVIOT
This Perthshire village, an ancient Pictish settlement, was chosen as his capital by Kenneth I when he united the Kingdoms of the Picts and the Scots. The ancient seat of the Scottish Kings of Dál Riata had been Dunadd in Argyll.

LINLITHGOW
The Palace of Linlithgow was a popular Royal residence, centrally located but removed from the mobs and diseases of Edinburgh. The Palace was in regular Royal use from the twelfth century and most of the Stewart Kings contributed to its rebuilding and refurbishment. Linlithgow was the birthplace of James V and Mary. It was James V's court at Linlithgow which witnessed the first performance of Lyndsay's *Ane Satyre of the Thrie Estaitis*.

PERTH

This richly endowed Royal Burgh occupies a strategic position at the head of the navigable stretch of the Tay. It was the location of a considerable number of Parliaments and Council meetings in the medieval period, and the Treaty ceding the Norse possessions in the Hebrides to Alexander III was signed here. The Dominican Blackfriars monastery was a favoured residence of James I. It was also the place where he was assassinated in 1437.

ST ANDREWS

When the supposed relics of the apostle St Andrew were brought to the ancient Celtic church of Kilrymont, the rise of this isolated settlement to its position as Scotland's religious capital was assured. Erected as a Bishopric by 906 it gradually won primacy over the other religious centres such as Dunkeld. The see of St Andrews achieved Archepiscopal status in 1472. As well as ecclesiastical associations it was also favoured as a Royal residence and James III was probably born in the Bishop's Castle.

SCONE

In any consideration of a claim to capital status, the coronation place of kings must be given some attention. Scone, on the outskirts of Perth, had been a Pictish centre and its church flourished under Kenneth I, becoming the repository of the Stone of Destiny, claimed by some legends to be Jacob's pillow (Genesis Chapter 28 verse 11). This numinous block of sandstone has now been used for the enthronement or coronation of Dál Riatic, Scottish, English and British sovereigns. Its significance to the sense of Scottish nationhood was clear to Edward I who removed it in 1296 to Westminster Abbey, where, in defiance of the terms of the Treaty of Northampton (1328), it still (perhaps) remains. Although the Stone was no longer there, it was to Scone, with its traditions and associations that Bruce rode in 1306, to claim the crown and place himself in the authentic Royal line extending back to the Kings of the Picts and the Scots. The last coronation at Scone was that of Charles II in 1651.

STIRLING

Scotland's strategic centre *par excellence* – a fact attested to by the number of significant battles over the centuries fought within sight of the Castle walls. Alexander I died in Stirling Castle in 1124. The Parliament which took over the government from John Balliol was held at Stirling in 1295. The stark strategic fortress was, under the

Stewarts, turned into a secure Royal Palace. It was the birthplace of James IV and Mary was crowned in the town's Kirk of the Holy Rude in 1543 as was her son James VI. The Chapel Royal was founded at Stirling in 1501 and a new Chapel within the Castle was created in 1594 for the magnificently stage-managed baptism of James VI's first son, Prince Henry. Sir David Lyndsay, describes the Royal associations of Stirling – using its poetic name of Snowdon or Snawden:

> Adieu, fair Snawden, with thy towers high
> Thy Chapel Royal, Park and Table Round
> May, June and July would I dwell in thee
> Were I a man, to hear the birdies sound
> Which does against thy Royal Rock redound.
> David Lyndsay, *The Testament and Complaynt
> of Our Soverane Lordis Papyngo* (1538)

INDEX

The index references are to the date entries where reference is made to the topic discussed. It should not be assumed that the date shown in the index is the date of the event. Many persons and events have multiple entries – thus for example Sir David Lyndsay's *Satire of the Thrie Estaitis* is indexed under 1540 (for its first performance) and under 1947 (in the context of an entry on the Edinburgh Festival).

1513, War of 1503: 1511: 1513
Aberfoyle 1690
Act of Security 1705
Adam, Robert, Architect 1767: 1774
Adamnan, Abbot of Iona 563
Africa & Scots 1879
Agricola, Roman Governor 84
Alba, Kingdom of 800: 843
Albany, Robert Duke of 1411: 1424
Albert, Prince Consort 1853
Alexander III, King of Scots 1263: 1286: 1289
Alexander, William, Statesman 1629
Anaesthesia 1847
Angles 800
Angus, King of Dál Riata 503
Anne, Queen of UK 1705
Antonine Wall 139
Antoninus Pius, Roman Emperor 139
Appin Murder 1752
Arbroath, Declaration of 1320
Architecture 1542: 1767: 1774: 1853: 1904
Argyll & Sutherland Highlanders 1854
Argyll, Marquis of 1645
Arrol, William, Engineer 1890
Art 1784:1823
Art Nouveau 1899
Athelstan, King of England 937
Athenia Ship 1939

Auld Alliance 1295: 1513: 1560
Australia and Scots 1809

Badenoch, Wolf of, *see* Wolf of Badenoch
Baird, John Logie, Scientist 1929
Baker, Benjamin, Engineer 1890
Balaclava, Battle of 1854
Baldwin, Stanley, Prime Minister 1924
Ballachulish 1752
Balliol College, Oxford 1412
Balliol, Devorguilla 1412
Balliol, John 1412
Balmoral 1853
Bank of Scotland 1695
Banking 1695
Bannockburn, Battle of 1286: 1314
Barbarian Conspiracy 139
Barbour, John, Writer 1314
Basilikon Doron, Book 1600
Beaton, David, Cardinal 1546
Beaufort, Joan, Queen of James I 1424
Belhaven, Lord, Statesman 1707
Bell, Henry, Engineer 1769: 1770: 1803: 1812: 1859
Bell, Joseph, Doctor 1893
Bernard, Abbot of Arbroath 1320
Berwick 1295
Bible 1603: 1690
Bing, Rudolf, Musician 1947

Birgham, Treaty of 1289

Bishop's Wars 1643

Bishopbriggs 1793

Black Dinner 1440

Black Watch 1739: 1854

Black, James Whyte, Doctor 1902

Blackie, Walter, Publisher 1904

Blackwood's Magazine 1817

Blantyre l879

Blind Harry, Chronicler 1305

Boece, Hector, Historian 1040

Bonhill 1748

Book of the Dean of Lismore 1512

Boswell, James, Writer 1494: 1725: 1740: 1773: 1807

Bothwell Bridge, Battle of 1679

Bothwell, Earl of 1566

Bouch, Thomas, Engineer 1879

Boulogne, Treaty of 1544

Boulton, Matthew, Industrialist 1769

Bowling 1790

Boyd-Orr, John, Academic 1902

Braes, Battle of the 1886

Braxfield, Lord, Judge 1793: 1894

Breda, Declaration of 1650

Bridei, King of Pictland 685

Bridgeness 139

Brisbane, Thomas, Colonial admin 1809

British Aluminium Company 1943

British Army 1739: 1854

British Broadcasting Corporation 1929

Broomielaw Harbour, Glasgow 1770

Brown, John, Shipbuilders 1934

Bruce, Edward 1314: 1316

Bruce, Family 1124:1289: 1306

Brude, King of Pictland 563

Brunanburgh, Battle of 843:937

Buchan, John, Novelist 1935

Buchanan, George, Writer 1582

Burns, Robert, Poet 1494: 1759:1786

Byron, Lord Poet 1824

Cadell family, Ironmasters 1759

Caledonian Canal 1803

Calgacus, Caledonian leader 84

Callaghan, James, Prime Minister 1979

Cameron of Locheil, Donald 1745

Cameron of Lochiel, Ewan 1743

Cameron, Clan 1752

Cameron, Richard, Covenanter 1679

Campbell, Arch Marquis of Argyll 1645

Campbell, Clan 1493: 1752

Campbell, Colin, Factor 1752

Campbell, Colin, Soldier 1854

Canada 1935

Canadian Boat Song, Poem 1817

Canals 1790: 1803

Candida Casa 432

Carberry Hill, Battle of 1566

Carbisdale 1645

Carlyle, Alex, Clergyman 1736: 1748: 1774

Carnegie, Andrew, Industrialist 1848

Carron Ironworks 1759: 1790: 1820: 1828

Carver, Robert, Musician 1568

Catriona, Novel 1752

Caulfeild, William, Soldier 1724

Celtic Church 432: 664: 800: 1093

Celtic FC 1888

Chambers, Robert, Publisher 1771

Charles Edward Stewart, Prince 1745: 1746

Charles I, King of UK 1618: 1629: 1633: 1638: 1643: 1645: 1650: 1822

Charles II, King of UK 1650: 1666: 1822

Charlotte Dundas Steamship 1759: 1812

Chartism 1832

Chepman, Walter, Printer 1507

Childe Harold's Pilgrimage, Poem 1824

Chloroform, Introduction of 1847

Christian I, King of Norway 1472

Churchill, Charles, Poet1761

Civil War 1643: 1645: 1650

Clearances, Highland 1807

Clerk Maxwell, James, Scientist, 1873

Clerk of Penicuik, Family of 1731: 1873

Clyde, River 1770: 1812: 1841

Clydebank 1934

Coal mining 1826

Cockburn, Lord, Judge 1820: 1832

Coffey Still 1494

College of Justice Act 1532

Colman, Abbot 664

Colonisation 1629: 1698

Columba, Saint 432: 563: 800: 1938

Comet, Ship 1803:1812

Commisioners for Highland Roads 1803

Company of Scotland *see* Darien Scheme

Comyn, John of Badenoch 1306

Confession of Faith 1560

Congregation, Lords of 1560

Constantine III, King of Scots 937

Cope, General John 1745

Cor, Friar John 1494

Corbeil, Treaty of 1295

Corrieyarack Pass 1724

Court of Session 1532

Covenant 1618: 1638: 1643: 1645: 1666: 1679

Cowton Moor, Battle of 1138

Craig, James, Architect 1767:1774

Cressingham,Hugh, English commander 1297

Crichton, Sir William, Chancellor 1440

Crimean War 1854

Crofters' War 1886

Crofting 1886

Cromwell, Oliver 1643: 1650

Cronin, A.J., Novelist 1879

Crowns, Union of 1503: 1603

Culloden, Battle of 1746

Cumberland, Duke of, Soldier 1746

Cunningham, George, Politician 1979

Cutty Sark, Ship 1869

Dál Riata, Kingdom of 503: 563: 664: 685: 800; 843

Dale, David, Industrialist 1785

Dalhousie, Marquis, Gov Gen India 1902

Dalkeith 1503:1822

Dalrymple, James, Jurist 1681

Dalrymple, John, Master of Stair 1692

Dalyell, Tam, General 1666

Dargai, Battle of 1854

Darien Scheme 1695: 1698: 1705: 1716

Darnley, Lord (Henry Stewart) 1566

David I, King of Scots 1093: 1124: 1138: l164

David II, King of Scots 1316

de Bohun, Sir Henry 1314

de Warenne, John, English general 1297

Declaration of Arbroath 1320

Defoe, Daniel, Writer 1731

Denny, William, Shipbuilders 1869

Depression 1934: 1938

Disarming Act 1724: 1747

Discipline, First Book of 1616

Disruption 1733: 1843: 1900

Donald, Clan 1164: 1493

Douglas, Earls of 1440

Douglas, Gavin, Poet 1522: 1568

Douglas, James, Scottish commander 1314

Doyle, Arthur Conan, Novelist 1893

Drumclog, Battle of 1679

Drumossie Moor 1746

Drunk Man Looks at the Thistle, Poem 1926

Dumbarton 1511: 1582: 1841: 1869

Dunadd 503:843

Dunbar, Battle of (1296) 1295

Dunbar, Battle of (1650) 1650

Dunbar, William, Poet 1503: 1507: 1522, 1568

Duncan I, King of Scots 1040:1065

Dundas, Henry, Statesman 1793: 1902

Dundas, Robert, Lawyer 1857

Dundee, Sack of 1650

Dunfermline 1848

Dunkeld 800: 843: 1390

Dunollie 503

Duns Scotus, Scholar 1412
Durham, Treaty of 1138 ˙

East India Company 1902
Ecgfrith, King of Northumbria 664:
  685
Edinburgh, Castle 1440
Edinburgh, City Guard 1736: 1768
Edinburgh, Festival 1947
Edinburgh, Greyfriars Kirkyard, 1638
Edinburgh, Holyrood Palace 1822
Edinburgh, Mob 1633: 1731: 1736
Edinburgh, New Town 1767: 1774
Edinburgh, Old Town 1767
Edinburgh, Register House 1774
Edinburgh, St Giles 1633: 1822
Edinburgh, Treaty of (1328) 1314
Edinburgh, Treaty of [1560] 1295:
  1560
Edinburgh, University 1893
Education 1616
Edward I, King of England 1286:
  1289: 1297: 1305
Edward II, King of England 1314
Edward IV, King of England 1493
Edward VII, King of UK 1898
Edwards, Owen Dudley, Academic
  1893
Electricty & Magnetism, Treatise on
  1873
Elgin 1390
Elgin, Earl of, Viceroy of India 1902
Elizabeth, Queen of England 1603
Elliot, Gilbert, Gov Gen India 1902
Emigration 1807
Encyclopedia Britannica 1771
Eneados, Poem 1522
Enlightenment 1740: 1767: 1771:
  1774: 1776: 1784:1797
Episcopacy 1633: 1638: 1643: 1666
Equivalent 1695
Erskine, Ebenezer, Clergyman 1733
Ewing, Winifred, Politician 1979

Falconer, Sir John, Lord Provost 1947
Falkirk, Battle of (1298) 1305
Falkirk, Battle of (1746) 1746

Ferintosh, Whisky 1494
Feudalism 1124
Fingal, Poem 1761
First Book of Discipline 1616
First Reform Act 1832
First Statistical Account 1791
Five articles of Perth 1618
Five articles of Queen Margaret 1093
Fleming, Alexander, Scientist 1902:
  1928
Fletcher, Andrew, Politician 1707:
  1716
Flodden, Battle of 1503: 1513
Football 1888
Forres 1390
Fort Augustus 1724
Fort George 1724
Fort William 1645
Forteviot 843
Forth & Clyde Canal 1759: 1790:
  1812: 1826
Forth Rail Bridge 1890
"Forty Hours" Strike 1919
Fowler, John, Engineer 1890
France 1295
Fraser, M Kennedy *see* Kennedy-Fraser
Free Church of Scotland 1843: 1855:
  1900
Freedom Come-all-ye, Poem 1854
Fulton, Robert, Engineer 1812

Gaelic 503: 1526: 1616: 1690: 1761:
  1768: 1909
Gallacher, William, Politician 1919
Galt, John, Writer 1817: 1832
Gartcosh Steel mill 1971
Geddes, Jenny 1633
General Assembly 1618: 1638: 1731:
  1741: 1843: 1938: 1988
Gentle Shepherd, Poem 1725
Geology 1797
George IV, King of UK 1494: 1822:
  1823
George Square Demonstration 1919
Gibbon, Lewis Grassic, Writer 1914:
  1926
Gillespie, Thomas 1733

Gillies, Robert Pearse, Writer 1817
Glasgow 1767: 1770: 1859: 1898: 1919
Glasgow Boys 1899
Glasgow School of Art 1899: 1904
Glasgow Style 1899
Glasgow University 1846
Glen Orchy 1768
Glencoe, Massacre of 1692
Glenshiel, Battle of 1719
Godred, Norse King 1164
Golbourne, John, Engineer 1770
Golf 1866
Gordon Highlanders 1854
Gordon, George, Lord Byron 1824
Govan Shipbuilders 1971
Govan 1938
Graham, James *see* Montrose, Marquis of
Graham, James Visc Dundee 1679: 1689
Grangemouth 1790
Great Michael, Warship 1511: 1513: 1522
Greenock 1769
Grieve, Christopher *see* MacDiarmid, Hugh
Gruoch, Queen 1040
Gudeman of Ballengeich 1542
Gunn, Neil, Writer 1926
Guthrie, Tyrone, Theatre producer 1947

Haakon IV, King of Norway 1263
Hamilton, Patrick, Reformer 1528
Hardie, Keir, Politician 1897
Harlaw, Battle of 1411:1493
Hawthorne, Nathaniel, Writer 1881
Heart of Midlothian, Novel 1736
Heath, Edward, Prime Minister 1971
Helensburgh 1812:1904:1929
Henderson, Hamish, Poet 1854
Henry I, King of England 1124:1138
Henry III, King of England 1286
Henry IV, King of England 1424
Henry V, King of England 1424
Henry VII, King of England 1503: 1603

Henry VIII, King of England 1544
Henryson, Robert, Poet 1568
Heriot, George, Financier 1695
Heritable Jurisdiction 1747
Highland Clearances 1807
Highland Host 1679
Highlands & Islands Development Board 1943
Hill House, Helensburgh 1904
Hogg, James, Writer 1817
Holmes, Sherlock 1893
Home Rule 1949: 1979
Home, Lord, Statesman 1979
Honourable East India Company 1902
Hopkins, Gerard Manley, Poet 1881
Hot Blast Process, Ironmaking 1828
Hume, David, Philosopher 1740
Hunter, John, Naval officer 1809
Huntingdon, Honour of 1138
Huntingtower, Novel 1935
Hutton, James, Geologist 1797
Hydro-Electric Power 1943

Ian Lom, Gaelic Poet 1645
Inchtuthill 84: 139
Independent Labour Party 1919: 1924
India and Scots 1902
Industrial Revolution 1759: 1769: 1785: 1790: 1826: 1828
Ingibjorg, Queen 1065
Inglis, John, Lawyer 1857
Inveraray 1752
Inverlochy, Battle of 1645
Inversnaid, Poem 1881
Iona 563: 664: 800: 843: 1773: 1938
Iona Community 938
Iron Industry 1759:1828
Irwin, Margaret, Trades Unionist 1897
Islay 1164
Isles, Lordship of 1493

Jacobitism 1689: 1692: 1715: 1719: 1724: 1739: 1745: 1746: 1747: 1752: 1768: 1822
James I, King of Scots 1124: 1411: 1424: 1490: 1493

James II, King of Scots 1490: 1493
James III, King of Scots 1472: 1493
James IV, King of Scots 1493: 1503:
    1507: 1511: 1568: 1616
James V, King of Scots 1503: 1513:
    1532: 540: 1542: 1544
James VI, King of Scots 1503: 1566:
    1582: 1600: 1603: 1618: 1629: 1822
James VII King of UK 1689: 1822
James VIII "Old Pretender" 1715:
    1719
Jekyll and Hyde, The Strange Case of,
    Novel 1894
Joan Beaufort, Queen 1424
John Balliol, King of Scots 1295: 1306
John XXII, Pope 1320
Johnson, Samuel, Writer 563: 1725:
    1740: 1747: 1761: 1773: 1784
Johnston, Tom, Statesman 1885: 1943
Joleta, Queen 1286

Kells, Book of 800
Kelvin, Lord, Scientist 1846
Kennedy, James Bp of St Andrews
    1440
Kennedy-Fraser, Marjory, Musician
    1909
Kenneth MacAlpin, King 843
Kidnapped, Novel 1752
Killearn 1582
Killiecrankie 1743
Killiecrankie, Battle of 1689
Killing Times 1679:1689
Kilmarnock Edition, Poems 1786
Kilsyth, Battle of 1645
Kirk o' Field, Edinburgh 1566
Kirk, Robert, Clergyman 1690
Kirkintilloch 1790: 1826: 1943
Kirkwood, James Clergyman 1741
Knox, John 1546: 1616

L'Angelier, Pierre Murder victim
    1857
Lachin y Gair, Poem 1824
Largo 1731
Largs, Battle of 1263
Laud, William, Archbishop 1633

Lauder, Harry, Entertainer 1950
Lauderdale, Duke of, Statesman 1666
Law 1532: 1681: 1747: 1857
Leadhills, Library 1741
Lennox, Norse, raid on 1263
Leslie, David, General 1645: 1650
Leven, Steamship 1841
Libraries 1725: 740: 1741: 1848
Lighthouses 1807
Lindesay of Pitscottie, Robert 1472:
    1511
Linklater, Eric, Novelist 1926
Linlithgow 1540
Linlithgow, Marquess of, Viceroy
    1902
Linwood, Motor car factory 1971
Lipton, Thomas, Retailer 1898
Lismore 1512
Literature 1522: 1526: 1540: 1542:
    1568: 1725: 1731: 1741: 1748: 1768
    1771: 1814: 1817: 1824: 1854:
    1881: 1893: 1894: 1947
Livingstone, David, Explorer 1871
Loch Katrine 1859
Loch Lomond 1881
Loch Sloy 1943
Logarithms 1614
Lollius Urbicus, Roman Governor
    139
Lords of the Congregation 1560
Lordship of the Isles 1164: 1411: 1512
Lorn, King of Dál Riata 503
Louis XII, King of France 1511
Lucknow, Relief of 1854
Lyndsay, David, Poet 1540:1542:1947

MacBeth, King of Scots 1040:1065
MacDiarmid, Hugh, Writer 1926
MacDonald, Alastair, Poet 1768
MacDonald, Alex, Trades Unionist
    1897
MacDonald, J. Ramsay, Prime
    Minister 1924: 1929
MacDonald, Margaret, Artist 1899
MacErc, Fergus, King of Dál Riata
    503
MacGonagall, William, Poet 1879

MacGregor, James, Dean of Lismore 1512
MacIan of Glencoe 1692
Macintyre, Duncan Ban, Poet 1768
MacIntyre, Robert, Politician 1949
Mackintosh, Charles Rennie, Architect 1899: 1904
MacLeod, George, Clergyman 1938
MacLeod, John, Doctor 1902
MacMhuirich, Bardic Family 1411: 1512
MacPherson, James, Poet 1512:1761
Macpherson, John, Gov-Gen. 1902
MacQuarie, Lachlan, Soldier 1809
Macqueen, Clan 1743
Macqueen, Eagan, Gillie 1743
MacQueen, Robert see Braxfield, Lord
Magnus, Earl, Saint and Martyr 1065
Maid of Norway 1286: 1289
Major, John, Scholar 1582
Makars 1522
Malaria 1902
Malcolm I, King of Scots 937
Malcolm II, King of Scots 1040: 1065
Malcolm III, King of Scots 1040: 1065: 1093
Malcolm IV, King of Scots 1164
Mar, 6th Earl of, Jacobite Leader 1715
Mar, Earl of 1411
Margaret Plantagent Queen 1286
Margaret Tudor, Queen 1503: 1603
Margaret, "Maid of Norway" 1286: 1289
Margaret, Queen & Saint 1093
Marjorie Bruce 1316
Mary of Guise, Regent 1544:1560
Mary, Queen of Scots 1544:1560: 1566
Maxton, James, Politician 1924
Maxwell see Clerk Maxwell
McCormick, John, Politician 1949
McKail, Hugh, Covenanter 1666
McShane, Harry, Politician 1914
Medicine 1847: 1902: 1928
Merchiston Castle 1614
Millar, Patrick, Landowner 1812

Minto, Earl of, Viceroy of India 1902
Mitchell, James L see Gibbon, Lewis G
Mitchison, Naomi, Novelist 1926
Moir, David MacBeth, Writer 1817
Monasticism 664: 1124
Monkland and Kirkintilloch Railway 1826
Monmouth, Duke of 1679
Mons Graupius, Battle of 84
Mons Meg 1822
Montrose, Marquis of 1638: 1643: 1645
Morris, Talwin, Designer 1904
Morris, Tom, Golfer 1866
Muir, Thomas, Radical 1793: 1820
Munro, Neil, Novelist 1848: 1878: 1888: 1894
Murdoch & Aitken, Engine Builders 1826
Murray, Lord George, Jacobite 1745: 1746
Murray, Sarah, Traveller 1770
Mushet, David, Ironmaster 1828
Music 1568: 1909: 1947
Myllar, Andrew, Printer 1507

Napier Commission 1886
Napier, John, Mathematician 1614
Napier, Robert Engineer 1770: 1841
National Covenant (1638) 1618: 1638: 1666: 1949
National Covenant (1949) 1949
Nechtansmere, Battle of 685
Neilson, James Beaumont, Ironmaster 1828
New Lanark Cotton Mills 1785
New Makars 1926
New Year's Day 1600
Newbattle Abbey 1503
Newberry, Francis H., Artist 1899
Newhaven 1511
Ninian, Saint 432
Nobel Prizes, Scottish winners 1902: 1928
Norse 800: 843 1065: 1164: 1263: 1286: 1472
North of Scotland Hydro-Electric

Board 1943
North Sea Oil 1472: 1975
Northampton, Treaty of 1314
Northumbria, Kingdom of 664
Not Proven Verdict 1857
Nova Scotia 1629
Nuclear Disarmament 1938

Oil Industry 1975
Old Kilpatrick 139
Oliphant, Margaret, Writer 1817
Original Secession 1733
Orkney 1065:1472
Ossianic Legends 1512: 1761
Oswiu, King of Northumbria 664
Owen, Robert, Philosopher 1785

Paisley 1316
Paris, Treaty of 1295
Parliaments, Union of 1705: 1707:
 1716: 1731
Paterson, William, Financier 1695:
 1698
Patronage, Church 1733: 1843
Penicillin 1928
Pennant, Thomas, Writer 1743
Pentland Rising 1666
Perth 1314: 1935
Perth, Five articles of 1618
Perth, Treaty of 1263
Philiphaugh, Battle of 1645
Picts 139: 563: 664: 800: 843
Pinkie, Battle of 1544
Plantation of Ulster 1629
Political parties 1832: 1885: 1897:
 1919: 1924: 1949
Porteous Riots 1736
Porteous, John, Soldier 1736
Presbyterianism 1633: 1638:1643:
 1666: 1689:1733:1843:1853:
 1900:1938:1988
Prestonpans, Battle of 1745
Printing, Introduction of 1507
Privy Council 1600: 1616
Public Health 1859

Queen Elizabeth, Ship 1934

Queen Mary, Ship 1934

Radical War 1820
Radicalism 1793: 1820: 1832
Raeburn, Henry, Painter 1823
Railways 1826: 1879: 1890
Ramsay, Allan, Painter 1784
Ramsay, Allan, Poet 1725: 1741: 1784
Ramsay, James, Landowner 1733
Ramsay, William, Chemist 1902
Randolph, Thomas, Earl of Moray
 1314
Rangers FC 1888
Ravenscraig, Steel Mill 1971
Reamon, Rev Paraic 1988
Reformation 546: 1560: 1582
Reid, Jimmy, Shop Steward 1971
Reith, John, Dir Gen BBC 1929
Relief Church 1733
Renfrew 1164
Rennie, John, Engineer 1811
Rent Strike 1914
Renton Football Club 1888
Renton, Dumbartonshire 1888
Restoration 1666
Revolution Settlement 1689: 1692:
 1733
Riccio, David, Courtier 1566
Richmond & Gordon, Duke of 1885
Roads 1724:1 803
Robert I, King of Scots 1305: 1306:
 1314: 1316
Robert II, King of Scots 1316: 1390
Robert III, King of Scots 1390: 1424:
 1743
Robinson Crusoe, Novel 1731
Roderick Random, Novel 1748
Roebuck, John, Industrialist 1759:
 1769
Roman Wall 139
Ross, Robert, Physician 1902
Rosslyn Chapel 1065
Rosyth Naval Base 1939
Rough Wooing, The 1544
Roxburgh 1440
Royal Bank of Scotland 1695
Royal Oak, Ship 1939

Royal Scots Greys 1854
Rullion Green, Battle of 1666

Saddell Abbey 1164
Salisbury, Treaty of 1289
Saltoun 1716
Schism, Papal 1412
Schools 1616
Science 1614: 1769: 1797: 1828:
  1846: 1847:1873: 1928
Scone 1306
Scone Abbey 1568
Scotch Education Department 1885
Scotland and Wales Act 1979
Scots Quair, Trilogy of novels 1926
Scott & Linton, Shipbuilders 1869
Scott, Walter, Writer 1689: 1736:
  1814: 1822: 1824: 1902: 1988
Scottish Football Association 1888
Scottish National Party 1949: 1975:
  1979
Scottish Office 1885
Scottish Renaissance 1926
Scottish Trades Union Congress 1897
Secession, Original 1733
Secret Commonwealth, Book 1690
Secretary (of State) for Scotland,
  1747: 1885: 1943: 1949
Security, Act of 1705
Selkirk, Alexander, Mariner 1731
Selkirk, Earl of 1807
Sellar, Patrick, Landagent 1807
Shairp, John Campbell, Poet 1768
Shamrock, Yacht 1898
Sharp, James, Archbishop 1679
Sheriffmuir, Battle of 1715
Shetland 1472
Shinwell, Emmanuel, Politician 1919
Ships and shipping 1698: 1705: 1759:
  1769: 1770: 1790: 1804: 1841:
  1869: 1898: I934: 1933: 1971: 1975
Sick Heart River, Novel 1935
Silver Darlings, Novel 1926
Simpson, James Young, Doctor 1847
Sinclair, Earls of Orkney 1065
Sinclair, Sir John of Ulbster 1791
Skibo Castle 1848

Smeaton, John, Engineer 1770: 1790
Smellie, William, Publisher 1771
Smith, Adam Philosopher 1740:
  1776: 1797
Smith, George, Whisky distiller 1494
Smith, Madeleine 1857
Smollett, Tobias, Writer 1748
Soccer 1888
Solemn League and Covenant 1643:
  1650
Solway Moss, Battle of 1544
Somerled, King of Argyll 503: 1164:
  1493
Somerset, Edward Seymour, Duke of
  1544
Soutar, William, Poet 1926
St Clair *see* Sinclair
St Andrews 800: 1546: 1582: 1886
St Andrews, Golf Club 1866
St Andrews, University 1412
Stair's Institutions 1681
Stair, Viscount, Jurist 1681
Standard, Battle of 1138
Stanley, Henry Morton, Journalist
  1879
Statistical Account, First 1791
Steam Engine 1769
Stevenson family 1807:1894
Stevenson, Robert Louis, Writer
  1752: 1894
Stewart Dynasty 1316
Stewart, Alan Breck, Soldier 1752
Stewart, Alex, Wolf of Badenoch
  1390: 1743
Stewart, Clan 1752
Stewart, Henry Lord Darnley 1566
Stewart, James of the Glens 1752
Stewart, Walter 1316
Stirling Bridge, Battle of 1297
Stirling Castle 1542
Stirling, James, Mathematician 1741
Strathclyde, Kingdom of 664: 685:
  800
Stuart, John McD, Explorer 1809
Surrey, Earl of 1513
Sutherland Highlanders 1854
Sutherland, Countess of 1807

Sutherland, Thomas, Shipowner 1837
Symington, William, Engineer 1812

Tacitus, Historian 84
Tanistry 1040: 1440
Tay Rail Bridge 1879: 1890
Taylor, Teddy, Politician 1979
Tears of Scotland, Poem 1748
Tel-el-Kebir, Battle of 1854
Television 1929
Telford, Thomas Engineer 1803:1859
Thatcher, Margaret, Prime Minister 1979: 1988
Theatre 1540: 1725: 1947: 1950
Theory of the Earth, Book 1797
Thin Red Line 1854
Thirty-Nine Steps, Novel 1935
Thistle & Rose, Marriage of 1503
Thomson, William, Lord Kelvin 1846
Thorfinn, Earl of Orkney 1065
Thrie Estaitis, Satire of 1540:1947
Todd, Alexander, Chemist 1902
Torphichen 1812
Tour through Great Britain, Book 1731
Trade Unionism 1897:1919
Treatise on Human Nature, Book 1740
Tweedsmuir, Lord see Buchan, John

Ui Neill, Irish Tribe 432
Ulster, Plantation of 1629
Ulva 1809
Union of Crowns, *see* Crowns, Union of
Union of Parliaments *see* Parliaments,
United Free Church 1900
United Presbyterian Church 1900
Universities 1846
Upper Clyde Shipbuilders 1971
Ure, James, Covenanter 1679

Veto Act 1843
Victoria, Queen of UK 1847: 1853: 1859
Vienna Secession Exhibition 1899

Wade, George, Soldier 1724: 1739: 1803

Wallace, William 1297: 1305
Wanlockhead Library 1741
Wardlaw, Henry, Bishop 1412
Wars of Independence 1286: 1295: 1297: 1305: 1306: 1314
Water Supply 1857
Waterfalls 1881
Waterloo, Battle of 1854
Watt, James, Scientist 1759: 1769: 1770
Waverley, Novel 1814
Wealth of Nations, Book 1776
Weir of Hermiston, Novel 1894
Westminster-Ardtornish, Treaty of 1493
Wheatley, John, Politician 1919: 1924
Whisky 1494
Whitby, Synod of 664
Whithorn 432
Whyte, James, Theologian 1988
Wilfrid, Saint 664
William II, King of UK 1689:1692
Wilson, Andrew, Smuggler 1736
Wilson, John, Publisher 1786
Wishart, George ,Reformer 1546
Wolf of Badenoch, AlexStewart 1390: 1743
Wolf, Last 1743
Wolfe, James, Soldier 1739
Wood, Harvey, Arts administrator 1947
Woodburn, Arthur, Politician 1949
Worcester, English ship 1705
Wordsworth, Dorothy, Writer 1741
Wordsworth, William, Poet 1881
World War One 1914
World War Two 1934: 1939: 1943
Wyntoun, Andrew, Chronicler 1297